Telling Your Story
Exploring Your Faith

Telling Your Story
Exploring Your Faith

Writing Your Life History
for Personal Insight and Spiritual Growth

by B. J. Hateley

CBP Press
St. Louis, Missouri

Library of Congress Cataloging-in-Publication Data

Hateley, B. J. (Barbara J.)
    Telling your story, exploring your faith.

    Bibliography: p. 114
    Includes index.
    1. Christian life—1960—   . 2. Autobiography—Religious
aspects—Christianity. 3. Storytelling—Religious aspects—Christianity.
I. Title.
BV4509.5.H32   1985   248   85-13307
ISBN 0-8272-3626-3

Manufactured in the United States of America

For Michael—
my child, my friend, my anchor,
my joy, my love, my gift from God

Acknowledgments

I am grateful to many people who have contributed to my personal, intellectual and spiritual growth over the years: to all my professors at USC, especially Don Miller and John Orr, for their excellent teaching, their guidance, and their interest in my work; to Jack Crossley, whom I love dearly and whose influence on my personal and professional life is more profound than he'll ever know; and to Valerie Paton, Linda Oku, Alva Cox, as well as Gary Gould, Mike Halloran, Leo Missinne, and Milton Stern for their encouragement, moral support, and cherished friendship. They share themselves abundantly with me, and I am nourished by their love

To Jim Birren I owe a very special debt of gratitude, for his steadfastness and loyalty as mentor, friend, and colleague. Many of the ideas for this book began in our research and teaching at USC; I have developed, modified, and adapted them for Christian spiritual development.

I also want to thank Herb Lambert, my editor, without whose consistent encouragement this book would never have been written.

An additional note of thanks goes to Claire Flint (who brought me to the Bel Air church) and the *many* people who have attended my classes over the years and shared their life stories with me. I have used numerous excerpts from their writings in this book and wish I could acknowledge each author. To protect privacy, I have omitted names.

My final and most important thanks go to my parents, Gloria and Ken Gallagher. I am grateful to Mom for her unconditional love and her spontaneous, generous spirit; I am grateful to Dad for the standards of excellence that he encouraged me to achieve. I love them both for all they've taught me and the love they've given me, each in different ways.

Contents

                                                              page
Introduction: How to Use This Book   9

Section I. Looking at Life   11

1. Why Write? The Usefulness of Life Histories   12
2. Creativity and Metaphor: Some Keys for
              Writing   17
3. Life Span Development: Children Aren't the Only
              People Who Grow and Change   23
4. Maturity and Mental Health: You Are Young
              Only Once, but You Can Be
              Immature Forever!   33
5. Pulling It All Together: Fulfillment, Integration,
              Life Review, Reconciliation, Owning
              Your Own Life   40
6. Prospects for Personal Change   46

Section II. Looking at *Your* Life   54

1. Your Life As a River   54
2. Your Family   57
3. The Role of Food in Your Life   61
4. Your Life's Work   65
5. The Role of Money in Your Life   69
6. Your Heroes   71
7. Your Health History and/or
              Your Body Image   74
8. Your Sexual Development and Your Changing
              Sex Roles   76
9. Your Experiences with Death   79
10. The Loves of Your Life   81
11. The Hates of Your Life   84

12. Your Moral Development 86
13. Time 90
14. The Meaning of Your Life 92
15. Your Life Line 95

Conclusion: The Future—Where Do You Go
                  from Here? 97

Appendix A: Suggestions for Use in Groups 101
Appendix B: A Sample Class Schedule 110
Bibliography 114
Notes 116

"A humble knowledge of thyself is a surer way to God than a deep search after learning . . . . It is better for a man to live privately and to have a regard to himself, than to neglect his soul though he should work wonders in the world."

                                    —Thomas a Kempis

Introduction

How to Use This Book

For several years now I have been teaching classes on life history writing at various churches in the Los Angeles area. The classes have been well attended and the results gratifying. Self-discovery is a popular activity today, leading to spiritual growth for many Christians. Life history is a way of learning more about yourself and learning more about God at the same time. The process combines personal growth with spiritual growth. People come to feel better about themselves, and stronger in their faith through the process of writing their life stories.

This book comes out of a desire to extend the benefits of life history writing beyond the classroom—to make the process available to everyone who desires new spiritual insights and personal development. You can use this book to write your own life story; you may use it in groups to share the fruits of your self-explorations; you may use it to work with family members or friends. It can be used by churches in new-member classes, confirmation classes, and small study groups. It can be used in pastoral counseling, and in seminaries for the training of counselors. It is a very adaptable process that can have a variety of uses and many positive benefits for people of all ages.

The first section of the book, "Looking at Life," contains ideas and tools that will help you understand your life better. You will learn how "development" is a lifelong process, not something limited to children and adolescents. You will explore several different "models" of development, so you can see which one best fits the way your life has unfolded. You will examine various concepts of the "self" while you come to some understanding of what your own "self" is like. You will look at "change"—all the changes you've gone through, both good and bad, and all the change you still have to look forward to.

You can read the first section of the book before you start writing your life story, or you can read these chapters while you are writing.

The second section of the book, "Looking at *Your* Life," contains chapters on many of the "themes" of life—family, health, money, food; life's work, sex, death, etc. These are the topics that you'll use to write your life story, to divide life into manageable parts, while at the same time seeing the inter-connections among all those parts.

Each of these chapters contains several writing exercises as well as a list of sensitizing questions. You should not try to answer every one of these questions. Rather, use them to stimulate your thinking, to recall old memories, old feelings. If one particular question triggers some important memory, go with it. Follow your memory where it takes you. These questions are to *stimulate* your thinking, not restrict it; so if you go off on a tangent, that's fine. Don't feel as if you have to stick with the questions.

How much you write really depends on you. A minimum of two or three pages on each topic is what I suggest for people who take my classes, but often they will write much, much more. They find that once they get started, one memory leads to another and they just keep on writing for hours. Sometimes it's hard to stop because there is so much to explore.

By all means, write as much as you want. If you want to write a complete autobiography, then you would write a whole chapter on each topic. If you don't want to write a whole book, then just write a few pages on each topic. And of course, the longer you have lived, the more you will have to write about. A person who is twenty or thirty simply will not have as much experience to write about as a person who is forty or fifty, or seventy or eighty.

The point of the book is to help you write your life story, and in the process to learn more about yourself, your faith, and your God. You should use the theme chapters in the second half to guide and stimulate your memories and your writing, and you should read the chapters in the first half to promote self-understanding and personal growth while you write.

Section I

Looking at Life

The two sections of this book coincide with its two goals—to learn about how human lives in general develop, and to explore how your own life in particular has developed. As we learn more about other people, we understand ourselves better. As we gain insight into our own growth, we are in a better position to appreciate the changes through which others go.

Each human being is unique. No two people have exactly the same life experiences, personalities, and feelings. At the same time, however, human beings are similar in many ways. They all live through childhood, adolescence, adulthood, middle age, and old age. They all experience love and loss, joy and sorrow, triumph and tragedy, strength and weakness. In other words, human beings are at the same time both unique and similar, different and yet alike. Each of us is a special child of God with a particular history, but we are also united by our common bonds of humanity, our common experiences.

This first section deals with human lives in general, while the second section will help you explore *your* life in particular.

1

Why Write?

The Usefulness of Life Histories

"I beseech You, God, to show my full self to myself."
—St. Augustine

Why Write a Life History?

People have many different reasons for wanting to write their life stories. Whenever I teach life history classes, I ask participants why they signed up for the class. Here are some of their responses:

"I am in the process of climbing out of a deep hole, and I feel this class will be the final push out."

"I want to look under the carpet at hidden meanings."

"I want to write my autobiography because of my present growing reunion with Christ. I hope the discoveries about myself can strengthen my faith."

"How to use autobiography for understanding and guidance."

"To be able to understand myself (spiritually) in written form."

"Clarify my thinking in relation to God, self, and others."

"I'm in the class because I want to get more comfortable with my past, with memories of my parents, etc."

"To better understand ME."

The life history process clearly appeals to people who are seeking insight into themselves, understanding of how their relationships with family and other people have affected their lives, deeper appreciation of the role their faith has played in their development, and a feeling of closeness to God. People want to explore their faith and strengthen their faith. They need to reexamine the things they were taught as children, to analyze how their values and convictions have changed, and to come to a clearer awareness and deeper appreciation for the spiritual foundations of their lives.

Of course, not everyone is motivated by spiritual or religious reasons. Some people write out of a need for confession—they find it cathartic, releasing tensions that they've been keeping inside. It's a relief, a cleansing experience, to write and get things out in the open.

Some people write for self-defense. They feel unjustly accused of something, and they have to write to get their side of the story heard, to set the record straight.

Some people write for money. Their life has been unusual or interesting, and they feel that a lot of people will pay money to read about it.

Others write out of a desire for immortality. They will live forever as generations to come read their life story. Their fame will live on.

Still others write because they need to deposit themselves someplace. They need to leave their lives somewhere. For example, a few years back, a postman who lived in Florida wrote his very interesting life story as a post-retirement project. When his thick manuscript was complete, he had to decide what to do with it. He didn't want to leave it with his children or family because there were things in there he didn't want them to know. He didn't want to leave it with his friends for the same reason. So he packaged it up and sent it to the Gerontology Center at USC, asking that it be put it in a place for safekeeping. Clearly he was motivated by a need to deposit his life somewhere, where he knew it would be safe, appreciated, and cared for.

Some people write because they want to be an inspiration to others. They want to be a shining example for others to follow.

Others are just the opposite. They write to deter other people. They write about a life lived badly, in the hopes of keeping others from making their same mistakes.

Some people write for aesthetic reasons. They have some artistic vision or message that they want to share with others.

And some write out of exhibitionism. They simply want to show off!

Others write out of a desire for order. I call these people "the closet-cleaners of life." They have to sort things out, put each item in its little pigeon-hole, put everything in order.

Many people are self-analyzers. They want to figure out what makes themselves "tick." They want to understand their psychological, emotional, and spiritual dynamics. They want to know what motivates them.

Most importantly, many people desire a sense of accountability for the stewardship of their lives. They want to be able to say "I own my life." Good, bad, successes, failures, strengths, weaknesses—it all adds up to a total life that people need to accept as their own.

In reality, most people probably have several of these reasons in mind when they decide to write their life stories. They want to understand themselves better; they want to see how all the pieces of their lives fit together; they want to leave a testimonial for their children and grandchildren. These people are achieving several different purposes when they sit down to write.

How Life Histories Are Used

The uses of life history are just as varied as the reasons people have for writing them:

Life histories are used in psychological research and in the development of theories of personality and human development. Life histories are both the source of and the testing ground for these theories. The test of any developmental theory is how well it helps you understand your own life—if it doesn't help, then the problem is probably with the theory, not with your life. We'll explore some of these different theories in another chapter and learn what different scholars have had to say about the way human lives develop over the life span.

Life histories are also used in therapy. They can help the counselor to diagnose a person's problems, and life history writing assignments can help people to work on their problems between counseling sessions. Weekly writings can be like "homework" in the counseling process.

An additional benefit of doing one's life history is that in the vast majority of cases the process increases self-esteem. We all tend to be our own worst critics. We are all too aware of our shortcomings and failures. We tend to forget about all our good points and our strengths. That's because the mind is a mismatch detector. It's always easier to see what's wrong than what's right! We see what's wrong in other people, but even more, we see what's wrong in ourselves. So we really don't recognize how much we've done, how far we've grown, and all that we've accomplished in our lives—*until* we do a life history. Then we say, "Gee, I really *have* done all right over the years! I've accomplished a lot. I'm not such a failure after all." And we have the written proof right in front of us!

Life histories are also wonderful resources for historians. Firsthand accounts make history seem alive and personal, while enlivening the commonplace details of life. In addition, it is interesting to discover that the "self" we talk about today did not exist in earlier times. The whole concept of self has changed radically over the centuries.

Life histories are a marvelous way of bridging the "generation gap," as they tend to enhance the feeling of continuity between the generations. Young people love to read the stories of older family members, to learn about life in another era, before computers, television, and men walking on the moon. Through the elders' eyes, younger people can capture a sense of times gone by—times that will never come again. Life histories make one aware of one's roots, one's heritage, one's family and cultural context.

I am reminded of a funny illustration of family traditions: One day a husband was watching his wife prepare a roast to put in the oven. She cut a good-sized piece off the end of the roast, put the roast in the pan, seasoned it, and placed it in the oven. The husband asked why she cut that piece off the end. She replied, "I don't know. That's the way my mother always did it." The wife phoned her mother to ask her why she always cut the end off the roast. Her mother replied, "I don't know. That's the way *my* mother always did it." So the mother called *her* mother to follow this up, asking why she always cut the end off the roast. "Simple," the elder mother replied. "My roasting pan was too small, so I always had to cut a piece off the roast to get it to fit!"

Aren't family traditions wonderful? You'll find it fascinating to explore the origins of some of your own family traditions and customs, who started them, and why.

For the individual who is writing, the life history process is useful for self-enlightenment, for learning new things about oneself. It helps you come to terms with the issue of control in your life. Do you feel that you exercise a lot of control in your life? Do you make your own choices? Or is life something that happens *to* you, out of your control? Do other people control your life? Do circumstances control your life? Does God control your life? How do you feel about it? All these are questions that you can answer through the life history process.

Life histories, then, are useful for the people who write them, and useful for the people who read them. Family members and friends enjoy them, while historians and psychologists use them in their professional work. Not only is the written product useful, the writing process itself is rewarding and helps a person put life events into perspective. It enables you to see the significance of your experiences, and to find meaning in life.

2

Creativity and Metaphor

Some Keys for Writing

"What is autobiography?
What biography ought to be."

—Longfellow

One of the most common things that keeps people from writing is their own fear of the writing process. "But I don't know *how* to write," they plaintively state. "I'm not even any good at writing letters, much less a whole life story! Can't I just *tell* you my story instead of writing it?"

Sure, you can tell me your life story instead of writing it, but the results won't be the same because it is the writing process itself which helps you so much. When you are writing, you are forced to spend some quiet time reflecting before you write; you have to organize your thoughts somehow to get them on paper; you have to slow down and really *think* about what you're writing.

It is through this slowing down and reflecting on your life's events that you gain new insights. You begin to see the connections in your life.

You shouldn't worry about turning out a literary masterpiece. That's not what life history is all about. Life history is about trying to capture part of your life on paper, in your *own* way, in your *own* words. It is your own words that best convey the tone and texture of your unique life. One of the most beautiful and powerful life histories I've read came out of a class I taught several years ago. It was written by a middle-aged woman who had contracted polio as a young woman, and her husband left her shortly thereafter. She summed up her experience in just five words: "He left me. That *bastard.*" What more was there to say?

In these five words she captured all her pain, anger, betrayal, frustration, and abandonment. It was a profound statement.

Likewise, your own statements should come naturally from your own experiences. Write from your heart, from your guts. Let your soul speak for itself. Let the ink flow like tears onto the pages. The simplest words often speak the most eloquently.

Here are some simple exercises you can try to "limber up" your writing and imagination:

Exercise #1: *Ten Words*

Quickly list ten words that describe yourself. Don't think too long about it. Just jot down the first ten words that come to mind when you think of yourself.

_____   _____

_____   _____

_____   _____

_____   _____

_____   _____

Now look at the words you've chosen. What kinds of words are they? Are they positive words? Negative words? What makes them negative? Can some of the words be both positive and negative? For instance, the word "sensitive" is a positive word for some people and negative for others.

If your words are mostly positive, does that mean you have a good self-image? Do you feel comfortable with both your positive and negative words?

What kinds of words did you choose? Mostly adjectives? Did you choose any nouns, like woman, man, mother, friend, child of God, etc.? Did you choose any action verbs to describe yourself? Running, jumping, playing, etc.? What does that tell you about how you think about yourself?

Did you choose any colors? Red, yellow, purple, black, etc.? What do those colors mean to you? If you did not have a color on your list of ten words, try to think of what color best describes your personality. Are you a blue person? Orange? Brown? What does your color mean to you? How does your color represent you? Maybe your red is angry; maybe your red is passionate. Maybe your brown is the richness of earth; maybe your brown is boring. Describe what your color *signifies*.

As you can see, the words you choose convey a lot about how you think of yourself. Be aware of your words. Are they accurate?

Exercise #2: *Your Name*

What's in a name? Plenty!

Your name is probably the most important word that describes you. How do you feel about your name? What does it signify to you? Does it suit your personality? Why or why not?

Have you ever wanted to change your name? Why? Did you do it? What did your new name signify that your old name did not?

My son once came home from nursery school when he was about four and announced, "I want to change my name." I was surprised, and asked him, "What's wrong with 'Michael'? That's a perfectly nice name." "I don't like it," he replied. "OK then. What do you want to change it to?" He puffed himself up like a big he-man and said, "Big Louie!"

I don't know exactly what he was thinking, but it was very clear that Big Louie conveys something that Michael never could in a million years!

What does your name convey? How do you feel about it?

Exercise #3: *Historical Figures*

If you could be any historical figure, who would you want to be? Think about it for a few minutes. You have all of history to choose from. Who would you want to be? A religious figure? A biblical figure? A political person? A great king or queen? A scientist? An artist? An explorer? A philosopher? Some person who was not well-known?

Why did you choose that person? What aspects of him or her do you admire or like? Is your person a man or a woman? What does that mean to you?

* * *

Part of the intent of these exercises is to give you some new ways of thinking about yourself. We all develop certain set patterns in how we think about ourselves. We develop certain "personal myths" and stories about who we are.

Part of what this life history exercise is all about is to give you some new ways to think about yourself. In order to encourage insight, we want to encourage creativity.

Two Different Ways of Thinking

One way of conceptualizing creativity is to consider two basic types of thinking—convergent thinking and divergent thinking. Convergent thinking teaches you that there is only one right answer. Convergent thinking is what you are taught in math, for example. There is only one right answer for 2+2.

Divergent thinking, on the other hand, means that there are lots of possible answers, any or all of which could be correct. Divergent thinking encourages "possibility thinking" and creativity. An example: How many uses can you think of for a barrel? Store flour or wine or pickles, use as a table or stool, cut in half and use as a planter, climb in and go over Niagara Falls, take it apart and use the hoops for hula-hoops, use the slats for skis, etc. . . . Try this exercise yourself, and see how many uses you can think of.

Children tend to be very good at divergent thinking, but it diminishes as they grow older. It's very likely that their schooling discourages their creativity, as many teachers are only interested in the "right" answers. Research indicates that art students tend to be very good at divergent thinking, while science students tend to be very good at convergent thinking. It seems to be an either/or choice for most people. The exceptions are students who are honor students in both art and science; they are good at both kinds of thinking!

There is some question about whether this is a sex-linked trait. Little girls are interested in pleasing others, so they get good at convergent thinking at an early age. Little boys are more independent, less interested in approval, and therefore more creative in divergent thinking. Unfortunately, this often gets them into trouble at school, since teachers reward right answers, not creativity.

Some Choices to Make in Writing

The life history process affords you a wonderful opportunity to play with words and forms and ideas to understand yourself in a more creative way.

Think again about the words you choose when you write. You can decide whether you want to write in the first, second, or third person. If you use the first person "I" when you tell your story, the approach is direct and personal. If you direct your story to the second person "you," what you establish is the reader's presence as well as participation. "You" gets the reader involved, and it establishes empathy. Use of the third person "he" or "she" puts some distance between you and your life story. One woman who took my life history class started off writing in the third person because, she said, she "didn't want to get emotionally involved" in the process. She obviously felt a little vulnerable in revealing herself. However, by the third class session, when she discovered how much fun everyone else was having, she switched to writing about herself as "I."

You can adopt a particular attitude toward your audience. You may want to establish a tone of intimacy, as you share your secrets, or you may write with disdain, or with respect. You might want to write only for your friends and ignore your enemies; or you might write to justify yourself to your enemies, knowing that your friends already love you!

The kinds of verbs and adverbs you choose also affect your story. Is it an active life or a passive life you portray? Use adverbs like "here" and "there" so your audience can locate themselves. Prepositions can give subtle directions. For instance, there's a difference between being "in" the house and being "at" the house.

You want to be aware of time in writing your life story. Your verbs and adverbs will indicate this. What things happened in the past? What things are non-past? What's in the future? What things are timeless or eternal? (The sun sets in the west. Jesus lives in my heart.) You can use words like "then," "now," "yesterday," and "today" to help measure time. You can also talk about things which began in the past, but are not yet complete, as well as ongoing activities.

You might use "degrees of possibility" (words such as "if," "certainly," "possibly") to indicate the relative certainty of events. Or you might use a disclaimer like "I think" or "it seems to me" or "in my opinion," which lets others know how accountable you are for your version of an incident.

Exclamations express your strong opinions! Questions can be used to gain intimacy or empathy. Both exclamations and questions reach out to your audience, drawing them into your story and making them feel close to you.

You can use long, complex sentences, or short simple ones, depending on what effect you want to achieve. However, your sentences should sound natural, not contrived and stiff. Your story should sound like *you*.

You should feel free to use metaphors whenever you like. The first assignment of this book is in metaphors—describing your life as a river, or a branching tree. Maybe your life is like a flower, unfolding from a mere bud into a full flower. Use some divergent thinking here to capture the essence of your life with a metaphor.

In an assignment on "Health and Body Image," one man described his body as a car. He said his fantasy body was a sleek Jaguar XKE, with lean lines, a powerful engine under the hood, responsive, finely tuned, a superb performance machine, sporty and sexy. In reality, he said, his car/body was really an old beat-up Ford, with some dings and dents here and there. He hadn't maintained it very well, didn't get checkups very often, and he'd fed it inferior fuel—but all-in-all it was a fairly reliable old car. It got him where he needed to go. He was actually pretty fond of his old car/body!

You might think of this metaphor in terms of yourself when you do the chapter on health. What kind of a car are you?

You can also consider the form in which you choose to write. You aren't limited to straight prose; you can write a poem instead! Try it. It'll give you a new feel for your life! You can write your life story as a letter to someone, someone who's living, or maybe someone who's dead to whom you'd like to communicate your feelings. Perhaps you want to write your life story as a series of letters to your children or grandchildren (real or hypothetical).

You can write your life story as a prayer, or series of prayers. Augustine wrote his entire autobiography as a prayer to God.

You might even write part of your story as a song, if you're musically inclined. Songs are powerful reminders of people and incidents and periods in our lives.

The bottom line is simply to write in ways that will best capture your life the way you've lived it. The focus here is on knowing how your life *felt* to you—what were the sights, sounds, smells, and textures?

Let yourself *go* when you write. Feel free to express your feelings, your reactions to life events. A little creativity can go a long way in unleashing new insights and deeper understanding.

3

Life Span Development

Children Aren't the Only People Who Grow and Change!

"My selfe am center of my circling thought,
Only my selfe I studie, learne, and knowe . . . ."
                                        -Sir John Davies

At one time it was commonly thought that people "developed" during childhood and through adolescence, but that development stopped when a person reached adulthood. Adulthood was supposed to be a relatively stable plateau that one reached in one's early twenties, after one "settled down."

We now know that this is not true. Adults continue to grow and change and "develop" throughout the entire life span. Gail Sheehy's book *Passages,*[1] which explains the "predictable crises of adult life," helped millions of people understand what scholars had "discovered"—that development is a lifelong process.

Development is a general term. It has to do with the description and the explanation of changes that individuals characteristically show as they advance in chronological age. There are various kinds of changes and kinds of development to consider:

There is *biological development,* which has to do with physical changes in the human organism. A developmental biologist is concerned with the functional capacities of a person in relation to his or her potential life span.

There is *social development,* which deals with the different social roles we occupy at different ages. As you advance in age, your roles change, and you take on new ones as you leave other ones behind.

Psychological development relates to your adaptive capacities. How you respond intellectually and emotionally to changing life circumstances falls within the psychological domain.

Moral development pertains to your decisions and your behavior concerning moral issues in your life. Moral development involves learning right from wrong and understanding justifications for moral behavior. Your development in this area is characterized by changes in complexity and ambiguity.

Your *spiritual development* involves a more fully realized relationship with the Transcendent, a progressive understanding of God. We often hear people use such phrases as "growth in Christ" or "walking with God," which imply a lifelong process of development in faith and spirit.

In your life all of these different types of development are going on simultaneously, and they continue through your whole life. While the growth is not equal in all these areas, it is always apparent in one aspect of life or another. You are constantly developing and actualizing more of your potential as a human being.

Your biological development will probably be most apparent to you when you write about your health and body image and also when you write about sexual development.

Social development will be foremost when you write about your family and your life's work.

Moral development is considered in a whole separate chapter in the second half of this book.

And your spiritual development will be a factor in all of the chapters you write in your life story. It will be an especially strong element when you write about the meaning of your life.

Psychological development is the primary subject of this chapter, and we will cover several major theories of development in an attempt to discover which one(s) best help you understand your life. Each theory will be summarized only briefly, since one could write a whole book on each.

Erikson's Task Theory of Development

Erik Erikson is probably the best-known developmental theorist to date (excluding popularizers, such as Gail Sheehy). He proposed a "task theory" of ego development, in which there are eight stages, each one representing a choice or a crisis (task) for the expanding ego.[2] Erikson asserts that the resolution of each task or crisis determines the future development of the personality:

Age	Task	Resolution
Early Infancy	Basic Trust vs. Basic Mistrust	Child must develop trust that his or or her needs will be met, and that the world is predictable and reliable. Successful resolution of task leads to hope and trust. Negative resolution of task leads to withdrawal and basic attitude of suspicion and mistrust.
Early Childhood	Autonomy vs. Shame & Doubt	Potty-training is usually a significant issue here. Child needs to learn to control body functions and establish autonomy from parents. Successful resolution of task leads to establishment of will and autonomy. Negative resolution leads to compulsive attitude and behavior.
Play Age	Initiative vs. Guilt	This is when the child is experiencing greatest muscular development and ability to move around. Should be allowed to explore and initiate independent action. Successful resolution leads to a sense of purpose and initiative. Negative resolution results in inhibition and guilt.
School Age	Industry vs. Inferiority	Child must be allowed to finish projects or products he or she starts. Well-meaning adults who intervene ("Here, let me do that for you.") undermine child's sense of competence. Successful resolution leads to competence and industry; negative resolution results in inertia and feeling of inferiority.
Adolescence	Identity vs. Identity Confusion	This is the critical period when the individual is becoming more certain of who he or she is, solidifying value systems, taking on clearly defined sex roles, establishing a sense of belonging, and developing ideas about a career. Successful resolution leads to fidelity and a clear identity; negative resolution results in repudiation of the self and others.
Young Adulthood	Intimacy vs. Isolation	The individual should be establishing significant relationships with partners for friendship, sex, competition, and cooperation. The central issue is establishing a relationship of mutuality with a person of the opposite sex, which serves to regulate the cycles of work, procreation and recreation. Successful resolution leads to love and intimacy; negative resolution results in excessive exclusivity and isolation.

Adulthood	Generativity vs. Stagnation	The individual needs to contribute to future generations, either through his or her own children or through activities such as mentoring, philanthropy, civic activities—all of which involve a giving of oneself and a sharing of experience with younger generations. Successful resolution leads to care and generativity; negative resolution results in rejection and stagnation.
Old Age	Integrity vs. Despair	At this time in life, the individual needs to find some basic acceptance of life as appropriate, inevitable, and meaningful. The task is coming to terms with one's life as it has been lived. Successful resolution leads to integrity and possibly wisdom; negative resolution results in disdain, despair, and fear of death.

Variations on Erikson

Evelyn and James Whitehead have followed this same eight-stage format in their book *Christian Life Patterns*.[3] They amplify Erikson's work in a fine manner, adding the spiritual and religious dimensions to life span development. They discuss such topics as: adult crisis as a religious passage, religious images of intimacy, invitations of the mid-years, religious generativity, rites of reconciliation at midlife, Christian meaning in mature age, contribution of mature Christians to the community of faith, and the sacrament of aging.

Numerous other researchers have described variations on the task theory of Erikson. Roger Gould, in his book *Transformations*, outlines six basic stages, each of which is based upon debunking the myths of childhood:[4]

At age 16-22, the issue is "Leaving Our Parents' World," and the major myth to be shattered is "I'll always belong to my parents and believe in their world."

Age 22-28 brings the realization that "I'm Nobody's Baby Now." One must get rid of the notion that "Doing things my parents' way, with willpower and perseverence, will bring results. But if I become too frustrated, confused, or tired or am simply unable to cope, they will step in and show me the right way."

Age 28-34 involves "Opening Up to What's Inside." The myths to be debunked at this age are: "Life is simple and controllable. There are no significant coexisting contradictory forces within me."

Ages 35-45 is the "Midlife Decade" and the myth is, "There is no evil or death in the world. The sinister has been destroyed."

Once one reaches age forty-five and has successfully shed the many myths of childhood, the period of 45+ ("Beyond Midlife") promises to be one of peace, contentment, and self-respect. As Gould says, "The life of inner-directedness finally prevails—I own myself."

I often recommend Gould's book to my classes because it is very readable, while at the same time thorough, and he is one of the very few developmental theorists who does justice to women's life patterns as well as men's. Many theorists have done their research on men, and their concepts do not apply well to women's lives.

Some Problems with Stage Theories

There are other notable authorities who have described various stage theories of human development, including Charlotte Buhler, Else Frenkel Brunswick, Robert Havighurst, and Daniel Levinson. If one compares them, they are all fairly similar to each other and to Erikson. The impression one gets from reviewing these theories is that it seems to be very important to be "on time" in terms of development. These theories are all linear; that is, growth is in one direction, and people move from one stage to the next. If you are a certain age and find yourself not at the "right stage" according to somebody's theory, then the natural inference is that something must be wrong with you—you are out of synch with the "normal" developmental time frame. In other words, you'd better be "on time," or you'd better have a good reason why you're not!

Social pressure and expectations tell us in many ways whether or not we're "on time." You're thirty-five and still a bachelor? You've been married eight years and have no children? We get very clear ideas about what other people expect us to be doing at various stages in life. You're twenty-seven and still living at home?

And how many times have we heard someone say, "Act your

age!" We expect different kinds of behavior at different ages, and we let others know when they don't do what we expect.

Having such stage theories is a mixed blessing. On one hand, they are very useful in helping us understand how our lives unfold, and they help us make sense of the changes we go through in our adult lives. People read Gail Sheehy and say "Oh, I'm not going crazy. I'm not weird. I'm just having a midlife crisis—it happens to everyone." We are comforted by the fact that we are not alone, and we feel somewhat "normal" when we find ourselves in the pages of such a book.

On the other hand, stage theories can become tyrants, yardsticks by which everyone must be measured. If I don't go through all these stages in the right order, then something must be wrong with me. I'm not on time or I'm not normal. We must be very careful not to adopt these theories blindly as universal or true for everyone. Do these theories apply to women as well as to men? Do they apply to people in other cultures and countries? Do they apply to various ethnic groups in our own culture? Or are they culture-bound and class-bound? Are they white, middle-class theories? And is life really that neat and linear?

I don't have the answers for these questions, but I do think they're important to keep in mind as we seek to find theories which help us understand our lives. There are concepts other than stage and task theories which might be more helpful. Perhaps life is more cyclical rather than linear. Or perhaps life is neither cyclical *nor* linear.

Maslow's Need Theory of Human Development

Another way of looking at development is to consider *need theory,* the most well-known of which is Abraham Maslow's hierarchy of needs:[5]

According to this view, the human organism is motivated by states of deficiency, by lacks or needs, and it moves to satisfy those needs. Physiological needs are the most basic biological needs and the easiest to satisfy, with little effort for most people. These include the need for water, shelter, food, oxygen, temperature regulation, etc. Once we have satisfied our physiological needs, we move to pay attention to our safety needs. With this level of needs, we must maintain an orderly, predictable environment, and we must make sure that we are not threatened in a physical or a psychological sense.

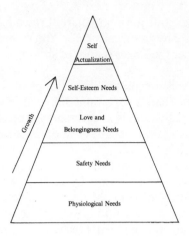

When we have secured our safety needs, we move to the next level—love and belongingness needs. This level concerns our need for human relationships, for mutual exchange of affection, for acceptance by a group, and for love and a sense of being wanted. According to Maslow, it is after we feel loved by others that we are able to begin meeting our self-esteem needs. We move from a need for love to a need for respect, from others and from ourselves. Included under self-esteem needs are achievement needs.

And finally, it is only after we have satisfied all of our lower-level needs that we can move to our need for self- actualization. Self-actualization means becoming whatever we are capable of, actualizing our full potential as human beings. It involves developing our identities through self-fulfillment, with an emphasis on each person's uniqueness and individuality.

Maslow states that very few people achieve self-actualization, and when they do, it is not permanent. There are moments or brief periods of self-actualization, but they are generally temporary. This is because we are always having to drop back to take care of some lower-level needs that aren't being met.

Maslow's hierarchy of needs has enjoyed great acceptance with psychologists and with the public in the past thirty years. Like stage theory, need theory has some pros and cons. One positive aspect is that it is somewhat less linear—you are moving up and down the hierarchy throughout your whole life. For instance, you may be working on your self-esteem needs, when suddenly you lose your job—so you're thrown back to satisfying safety needs and physiological needs. You're probably never at any level permanently. There is a lot of shifting and movement in this system.

In Maslow's scheme, personal development is more internally motivated rather than programmed by societal expectations. Therefore, each individual is progressing according to his or her own unique internal timetable of development rather than by an external standard.

One of the potential problems with Maslow's theory is that it too easily can become narcissistic. Individuals who are striving to become "self-actualized" may become exclusively concerned with their own needs, and turn into selfish, self-centered elitists. Christopher Lasch documented this tendency on a large scale when he wrote about the "me-generation" in *The Culture of Narcissism*.[6] People who become excessively concerned with their own needs run the danger of insensitivity to the needs of others. Maslow presents an interesting theory of human motivation and development, and it is useful for many people in understanding their lives, but there are still other theories to consider.

Other Ways to Explain Change and Growth

One such theory is the dialectic theory of human development, which asserts that personal growth is the result of tension and conflict between polar opposites within the individual.[7] That is, personality characteristics come in pairs, such as masculine/feminine, openness/closedness, altruism/aggression, competition/cooperation, isolation/community, stability/change, etc. These opposing characteristics exist in everyone, and we are always struggling to keep them in balance. The relationship between these characteristics is always dynamic and changing, not stable. Therefore, the natural state of the organism is tension, struggle, and conflict. There are no stages to finish or tasks to resolve. In fact, in this concept, nothing is ever resolved on a permanent basis! Life is never in balance for very long.

The dialectic analyst says that we spend our whole lives struggling to respond to opposite impulses or desires. For instance, the classic juggling act that many people have to handle in dealing with work and love, career and family, professional life and personal life. You pay attention to your job and career so that you feel you're doing a good job. Then the people in your personal life start letting you know that you're neglecting them. So you spend more time with your family and friends, and you begin to get signals that you're neglecting work. You can never win!

The dialectician will tell you not even to try to win. The nature of life is conflicting demands, so you should simply learn to cope with the tension and the continual struggle with opposites. The dialectic approach to life-span development assures us that there are no "pat" answers to life's dilemmas, that we are all constantly in a state of flux and changing every day.

It is precisely this emphasis on change that is so appealing. For if we are always struggling with work and love, privacy and community, independence and dependence, then there is constant potential for growth. Every day holds possibilities for creative living and a fresh approach to problems.

One of the main contributions the dialectic approach makes to self-understanding is the awareness that human life is dynamic and changing, that conflicting feelings and ambivalence are natural. If one is more aware of these natural tensions and conflicts, one can approach life with more understanding, flexibility, tolerance, and perspective.

A dialectic view of life helps many people feel more relaxed and accepting of the opposites in their lives. If they can see these opposites as "normal," they can quit trying so hard to nail things down.

But the ultimate test for the dialectic theory of human development—and for stage theory, task theory, need theory, or *any* theory—is the question: Does it help you understand *your* life? Does it make sense in the context of your life? Does it fit your experience?

Theories, after all, are not handed down from on high. Developmental theories are derived from the study of many people's lives. Maybe the general patterns are true for most people (maybe!), but they may not be true for you. These theories should be read as descriptive, not prescriptive. Do not interpret them as saying your life *ought* to develop like theory A, B, or C. A theory of human development is a tool which should help explain behavior and promote self-understanding. It should not be used as a blueprint by which everyone should live.

If one of these theories presented here is helpful to you in making sense of your life experiences—great! If these theories don't fit your life, then disregard them. They are simply tools, and some tools are more useful than others, depending on your situation.

If these theories are not helpful, maybe you could even make up your own theory about how you think human lives develop. Who knows? Your theory might be a tremendous help to future life history writers trying to figure out the puzzle of their lives!

4

Maturity and Mental Health

You Are Young Only Once, but You Can Be Immature Forever!

In chapter 2 you listed ten words that describe yourself. You then analyzed those words to see how much of your "self" was really revealed there, in order to discover if there were aspects of yourself that needed exploring.

In this chapter, as we enter a discussion of maturity and mental health, I'd like to try one more exercise in metaphor to further your journey into your "self."

Exercise: *Fantasize yourself as an animal:*

Step 1: If you could be *any* kind of animal, what kind of an animal would you be? _____

Step 2: If I were to ask the people who know you, your friends and family, what sort of an animal would they say you are? _____

Step 3: Since you know yourself better than anyone, what kind of an animal do you think you *really* are? _____

Now look at the three animals you have chosen. Are they very different from each other? Are they similar kinds of animals? Did you choose the same animal each time? What sorts of qualities do your animals represent? For instance: Tigers or lions usually imply power, beauty, courage, and freedom. Otters mean playfulness, curiosity, freedom, fun, energy, and lovableness. Different animals represent different qualities.

What are the qualities you aspire to have, as implied by your first animal choice?

What are the qualities that other people see you as having, the qualities of the animal in your second choice?

And what are the qualities that you *really* think you have, according to your third animal choice?

When you link all three choices together, what you have is three different aspects of your "self." You could sketch it to look something like this:

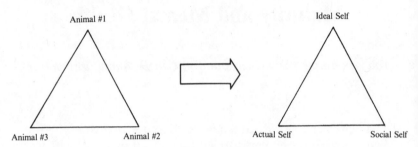

The first animal you chose represents your ideal self, the kind of person you would *like* to be. This is the vision or the goals that you hold for yourself as a person. These are the qualities that you would like to have.

The second animal choice represents the way other people see you. Your social image is the way your family and friends and co-workers view you. These are the qualities that other people say you have.

The third animal choice represents how you see yourself. This is not the self you'd *like* to be; this is the self you really are today. This is the self you see when other people aren't around. This is what you see as the "real you."

As you look at this three-part sketch of yourself, do you see any big discrepancies? Are there major differences, for instance, in the way you see yourself and the way others see you? If so, your triangle of self would look something like this:

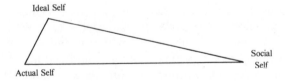

The triangle is distorted. The social self is a long way from the actual and ideal selves. This kind of person always feels misunderstood, always feels that other people don't really know him or her.1. It's a painful feeling, a lonely feeling, a feeling of being isolated from others. This is a common problem with adolescents (although certainly not limited to adolescents), who often complain that their parents don't understand them. "My family doesn't know who I really am," they complain, "Nobody understands me."

Another kind of self might look like this:

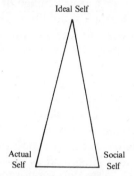

Ideal Self

Actual
Self

Social
Self

This is the idealist, the perfectionist. This is the person whose ideal self is very different from his or her actual self. This is the person who is always disappointed in himself, who always falls short of his ideals. He's never satisfied, rarely happy with himself. He may often be filled with self-disgust and self-loathing, because his actual self falls so far short of his ideals. This is also a painful, isolating feeling.

Anytime there is a distortion in the triangle of self, the person feels tension and discomfort. The reasonably healthy self should look something approximately like this:

Ideal Self

Actual
Self

Social
Self

There is roughly equal distance between each pair of aspects of self. There needs to be a healthy distance between ideal and actual, so that the person has opportunity to grow and develop toward his ideals; but there should not be so much distance that the ideals become unrealistic and unattainable. Otherwise, the person would always feel like a failure.

Likewise, there should be a healthy distance between the social self and the actual self, so that there is some room for privacy; but there should not be so much distance that the person feels misunderstood all the time. Your image of yourself needs to be fairly similar to other people's image of you.

And finally, the ideal self should be a personal concept which is not totally at odds with the ideals of one's social context but at the same time should do justice to the person's unique values and beliefs.

If the triangle of self is roughly equal in its dimensions, as above, then the person's sense of self is well integrated. It fits together comfortably. There should not be a great deal of tension between the various aspects of one's self.

Current personality research indicates that one's "self" naturally becomes more integrated as one grows older. Life has an integrating effect on the personality. The triangle becomes tighter, and the three aspects fit together better as one ages. The three corners move closer together because of one's life experiences:

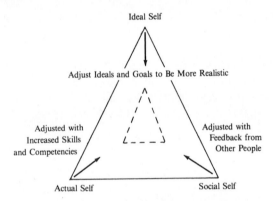

You adjust your ideals to a more realistic level. The idealism of youth gives way to the realism of the mature adult. The social self changes as you get more feedback from other people and you learn how you come across to others. Your social self adjusts with continual feedback. And your actual self changes as you develop new skills and master all the elements of your life. The three aspects of self become more congruent as life experiences have an integrative effect.

This is true for most, but not all people, as they age. They come to know themselves better, and they accept themselves for what they are. Their sense of self becomes more clearly defined and comfortable. This is the reason people often say, "I'd never want to be a teenager again," or "What? Go back to being twenty-five again? Forget it! At forty I'm happier than I've ever been in my life!" For the majority of people, self-understanding and self-acceptance are the satisfying fruits of years of experience.

It is this same self-understanding and self-acceptance that are key components in mental health. Mental health is much more than simply the absence of mental illness. It has to do with the ability to deal with the issues of life in an effective and satisfying way. Mental health is characterized by a feeling of contentment or satisfaction with the way you have lived or are living your life. It usually also means that you have come close to living up to your ideal self.

Jahoda, in 1958, outlined a list of criteria of mental health which is widely accepted.[8] It includes:

—positive self attitudes
—growth and self-actualization
—integration of personality
—autonomy
—reality perception
—environmental mastery

The basic underlying notion here is that mental health involves the maximizing of one's personal *potential* and capacities. Being mentally healthy means being all that you can be!

In very simple terms, a mentally healthy person can say to himself or herself:

—"I am." (integration)
—"I will." (self-intent)
—"I can." (self-mastery)
—"I accept myself." (self-regard)
—"I accept my life as I have lived it." (ideal self)

Maturity

What, then, is maturity, and how does it relate to mental health? Maturity implies fullness of growth, the blossoming of a fully-developed human being. While developmental psychology has shown us that personal growth is a lifelong process, there is usually some point in life when you feel you have reached "maturity." For many, this point comes sometime during middle age, in the thirties, forties, or fifties.

In 1977, George Vaillant conducted a study of what he called "successful middle-agers" and he discovered certain characteristics which they all had in common:[9]

1. They knew how to conserve energy. That is, they knew how to pick their battles and how to conserve their emotional and psychic energy by not jumping into every battle that life presented. They knew how to be flexible and adaptable, so they weren't emotionally devastated by every problem.

2. They knew how to confront other people when the issue wouldn't go away. They didn't ignore problems; they dealt with them directly and effectively.

3. They knew how to use people, how to delegate responsibility, and how to share the work. They understood that other people are resources and that it is OK to call upon their services to get things done.

4. They had learned how to rely on experts for advice. Just as you don't have to *do* everything yourself, you don't have to *know* everything yourself. Effective use of experts can save you time as well as energy.

5. They built on their past experiences of success. By using successful past experiences as the foundation for future endeavors, they found their chances for continued success much higher.

Successful people aren't defined necessarily by material success, although that can be one measure. What is more important for our discussion here is success in personal and interpersonal terms. The successful mature person takes responsibility for his or her life, responds to situations appropriately, solves problems effectively, and maximizes personal resources. They make the most of themselves, and they make the most of life!

Wisdom

We cannot leave this chapter on maturity and mental health without some mention of that elusive treasure—wisdom. Wisdom is certainly more than experience. We all know people who've had lots of experience, but never seem to learn from it! We wouldn't call them wise!

Experience is one component of wisdom, but in addition, one must be able to generalize from experience. One must distill one's experiences, interpret their meaning and significance, and integrate the experiences with other experiences. The process of generalization takes time and reflection. It requires clear thinking and analytic skill.

The wise person is also able to discern critical issues. Every issue is not of equal importance—some are critical, some are inconsequential. The wise person understands this and has the power to discriminate among life's issues. This is partly intuition, partly logic. The intuitive aspect gives one a "sense" that a problem is critical, while at the same time logic enables one to spot critical issues on the basis of their potential consequences.

The wise person is also characterized by emotional control and balance. He or she is not wiped out by a flood of feelings from every event. The wise person *feels* things, but has a good control of those feelings so they don't become overwhelming or devastating.

And finally, the wise person has a sense of perspective. Wisdom involves understanding the overall picture, where one's place is in this picture, and a sense of proportion that enables one to react appropriately to life issues. This implies a certain emotional distance and the ability to step back from issues to see them in better perspective. If you are caught up in the middle of a problem, it is very difficult to keep your sense of proportion and react wisely. You must have the ability to step outside of yourself and to step outside of the situation to see the whole picture.

Wisdom, maturity, and mental health—despite the elusiveness of precise definitions—are issues to keep in mind during the process of writing your life story. Coming to terms with your life as you have lived it, accepting responsibility for your life and its consequences, discerning the critical issues in your development—in these ways you are contributing to your own mental health, maturity, and wisdom.

5

Pulling It All Together

Fulfillment, Integration, Life Review,
Reconciliation, Owning Your Life

"Know Thyself"—Delphic Oracle

When you're writing your life story you're basically looking at three things: (1) the events in your life, (2) your feelings and subjective reactions to those events, and (3) the achievements or products of your life. The outcome of this self- examination process is what psychologists call personal integration, or personality integration. You take the masses of details in your life, all the events and your reactions, and from them you can make some generalizations about yourself. You can come up with some general concepts about the kind of person you are.

You recall one event, and that memory leads to another memory, and another, and so on. It's a process of association, where you see how one life event is connected to another. This process of association shows you how things are tied together, linked not only in your memory but in reality. As you think through your life, the events become more connected than ever— they are almost knitted together into what you might metaphorically call "the fabric of life." You can follow the threads of your life; you can see the patterns, the general directions of events. You can appreciate the texture, the colors, the subtle tones here and there, the way everything is woven together. Some might even call it "the tapestry of life" because of life's richness and substance. Tapestries tell a story.

What you see through this process, then, is that all those life events, all those details, all those memories add up to something—a total person. You might think of it as putting a jigsaw puzzle together—each piece has its place in the total picture of your life.

40

While the product of this endeavor is integration (a feeling of wholeness, connectedness), the process itself is called "life review." Robert Butler, a psychiatrist well-known in the field of aging, coined the term "life review" to describe the process of reminiscence he saw so often in his elderly patients.[10] Unlike most people who condemn this tendency of older people to "live in the past," Butler saw that this process of reviewing one's life to be a normal, healthy activity for people in advanced years. This is the time in life when they should be reviewing their lives, putting events into perspective, working through unresolved conflicts and emotions, and finding meaning in life events.

It's easy to see how this idea of life review ties in with Erik Erikson's last stage of life, "integrity vs. despair." In order to live with integrity and peace of mind at the end of life, one should spend time reviewing life events to better understand them and to come to terms with one's destiny.

In talking about the importance of life review, Butler outlines what happens if one *doesn't* do a life review:

1. One will feel a sense of meaninglessness; one will depreciate one's self as well as one's past.

2. There will be the persistence of unresolved conflicts, unresolved anger over past hurts. In addition, one will be unable to reconcile one's hopes with the reality of one's life as it was lived.

3. One will have a less complex, less rich view of the past; one will be less flexible in viewing the self and the past; one will see life from a very narrow perspective.

4. One will have persistent feelings of grief in relation to the losses of one's life.

5. Failure to do a life review will lead to feelings of rejection, social isolation, and alienation.

It is clear from Butler's work that people who deny the past or ignore it will suffer from psychological and emotional problems in later life. His work demonstrates that it is crucial to come to terms with your past, to spend time exploring your life history and understanding how and why things developed as they did.

By and large, most people don't want to relive their lives; they just want to tidy up a few things, to tie up a few loose ends. This is what integration is all about. Most people do not regret what they did in life; more often, they regret what they *didn't* do. They wish they'd taken advantage of opportunities, taken more risks.

Taking Stock at Various Stages in Life

While Butler's work focuses on the importance of life review for older people, I would expand the notion to include people of all ages. The urge to "take stock" of one's life is not limited to any particular age group. The retrospective impulse, the need to look back and reflect on one's life, can occur at a very early age and again any number of times during an individual's life.

Many things can trigger a life review—a change in lifestyle, a significant transition or turning point, career changes, births, deaths, weddings, graduations, divorces, etc. Significant holidays, especially Christmas and Easter, make one feel the urge to reminisce, especially about family. Certain birthdays which mark a rite of passage (sweet sixteen, coming of age at eighteen or twenty-one, the beginning of a new decade at thirty, or forty, or fifty, or the symbolic age of retirement at sixty-five) can turn one's thoughts to the past. Any event which disrupts the normal routine of day-to-day life can cause one to engage in life review. Any turning point or major beginning or ending in life activities triggers the urge to spend some time reviewing life's progress to date. The impulse to take stock is especially strong during times of transition or change.

Young people often feel the need to assess where they've been before deciding where they're going, as they prepare to launch into new worlds of college, career, marriage, and family. This is a time of uncertainty, as the young adult leaves the freedoms of childhood behind and contemplates the adult responsibilities that lie ahead, realizing that one's life is increasingly in one's own hands.

Middle-aged people find life history especially helpful, as they go through various mid-life transitions and "crises"— assessing themselves, their careers, their relationships and families, and their value systems. Children leaving home, career changes, new health problems, strained marital relationships, vague feelings of restlessness, disillusionment with current goals and lifestyles—all prompt the middle-ager into looking back where he or she has been, before setting new directions for the future years. Many individuals who lament that their cup is half empty, upon closer examination of their lives, joyfully discover that the cup is still half full!

Older persons also find the process of life review to be fruitful, as they finish careers and relinquish previous roles. Theirs is the task of reviewing decades of experience, integrating often discontinuous life events, and finding meaning in existence. They are often surprised to discover the experience, knowledge, and wisdom that their lives contain. They find that all those years add up to something—a total person. They find significance; life *means* something!

What Christians Learn During Life Review

The life review process is especially significant for Christians who are searching for answers, who may be experiencing struggles or crises of faith. A life review can help them to see God at work in their lives, to see the miracles they have experienced, the grace which envelops them, the hope and promise that are available to them.

Undoubtedly the most important result of doing a life review or a life history is the feeling of *reconciliation*— reconciliation to your past; reconciliation to other people (often even people like parents or older family members who have died, leaving you with "unfinished business" and unresolved conflicts); reconciliation to yourself (accepting the previously unacceptable aspects of yourself); and reconciliation to God, from whom we sometimes feel estranged. Writing your life story provides you with the opportunity to achieve reconciliation in all aspects of your life, to leave old emotional baggage behind, and to come to a new, deeper understanding of your life and your faith.

Reconciliation is especially important in coming to terms with the negatives of your life, the "bad" parts of yourself. Love, by its very nature, is unconditional. If you love someone when they're good, but withdraw love when they're bad—then you're not really loving. Love is steadfast and unconditional. God's love sets the standard.

Think about the way you love other people. Do you love them consistently, whether they are good or bad? Do you make it clear that you always love the *person,* even though you may not like that person's *behavior* on occasion?

And are you able to do the same for yourself? Can you love yourself, even when you're not always good? This is a very difficult thing for many Christians. We find it difficult to accept God's unconditional love because we cannot love ourselves. We cannot forgive ourselves for our shortcomings, so we find it hard to believe that God forgives us and loves us. The struggle for self-acceptance is a difficult one.

Often the struggle has its roots in the ways we were reared as children. Some children are reared with guilt, and others with shame. The child who is brought up with guilt is made to feel responsible for other people's happiness. "How could you do that to your sister?" "How could you disappoint your father like that?" "Look how upset you've made your mother!" "You've broken your mother's heart!" These are the things a child reared with guilt hears. The child grows up feeling a heavy burden, for the happiness of other people is dependent on his or her good behavior.

The child who is reared with shame is made to feel that something is intrinsically wrong with him or her. "What's the matter with you? Can't you do anything right?" "You're so lazy! How do you expect to amount to anything?" "Look at this room— it's a pig pen! How can you live like such a slob?" These are the sorts of things a child reared with shame hears. The criticisms are personal and hurtful. They attack the child's basic character, making him feel that he is somehow defective and worthless. Because he always heard what a terrible person he was, this child grows up with a marked lack of self-esteem and self-confidence.

Think about the way you were reared, and the way you in turn reared your own children. Were you brought up with guilt or with shame? Many people report that they were reared with *both!* They felt responsible for their parents' happiness, *and* they felt somehow inadequate as persons. Using either guilt or shame on a child is a very destructive way of disciplining and shaping behavior. Both methods inhibit the development of a healthy sense of self and can result in a crippling lack of self-confidence. This kind of damage is extremely difficult for someone to undo later on. The early conditioning is very powerful.

Because of such childhood training, many adults have trouble with self-acceptance, which in turn makes them doubt God's acceptance. They want very much to be accepted and loved, but because they never experienced such love as children, they don't know how to respond when acceptance and love are offered through Christ. Ultimately, it's a vicious cycle which is difficult to break.

Writing a life history can be helpful in breaking this cycle because it gives you an opportunity to put your life events in new perspective. You can write about childhood problems and old hurts, and you can work through some of your unresolved feelings. You can stop listening to those parental voices from the past and assess yourself as an adult. You can form your own opinion of what kind of person you are and not be so worried about other people's opinions. You can feel more confident of your abilities and more comfortable in the knowledge of who you are.

Life history also provides you with a way to find significance and meaning in your life events. It is absolutely critical that we, as human beings, find some meaning in our lives. Without it, life is empty, pointless, futile. Sooner or later, we must all deal with the existential questions, "What does it all mean? Why do I exist?"

Viktor Frankl founded a branch of psychotherapy called "logotherapy," which is designed specifically to help people find meaning in their lives. Frankl says that while the "will to meaning" is the same in every person, the meaning itself is different for every person. Some people find their meaning in their children, others in their work, still others in art or creation or nature or religion. And the meaning of a person's life can change over time—there is not one absolute meaning for a person. His own words express it best:

> The meaning of life differs from man to man, from day to day and from hour to hour. What matters, therefore, is not the meaning of life in general, but rather the specific meaning of a person's life at a given moment. . . . One should not search for an abstract meaning of life. Everyone has his own specific vocation or mission in life; everyone must carry out a concrete assignment that demands fulfillment. Therein he cannot be replaced, nor can his life be repeated. Thus, everyone's task is as unique as is his specific opportunity to implement it.
>
> As each situation in life represents a challenge to man and presents a problem for him to solve, the question of the meaning of life may actually be reversed. Ultimately, man should not ask what the meaning of his life is, but rather must recognize that it is *he* who is asked. In a word, each man is questioned by life; and he can only answer to life by *answering for* his own life; to life he can only respond by being responsible. Thus, logotherapy sees in responsibleness the very essence of human existence.[11]

Writing your life history provides you with the opportunity to answer for your life, to clarify for yourself what your life means, and to establish your own responsibility. You needn't look to others to tell you what life is all about.

6

Prospects for Personal Change

"We may come to think that nothing exists but a stream of souls, that all knowledge is biography, and with Plotinus that every soul is unique." —W.B. Yeats

Character is fate. Or is it? Some people, when they run into trouble in relationships, say, "That's just the way I am. Take me or leave me." They sound as if their personalities were set in concrete, not capable of changing. Is that true? That's the question we'll be discussing in this chapter.

Klaus Riegel, a famous psychologist and philosopher, says that the mature person is one who can handle the "dialectical nature of reality."[12] That is, the mature person is one who can live with the tension generated by opposite dimensions in life—independence vs. dependence, masculine vs. feminine, intimacy vs. privacy, community vs. individuality, career vs. family. Another such dialectic is stability vs. change. We need both in our lives. Too much stability would be boring and mind-numbing; too much change would make us feel anxious, insecure, and unsettled all the time. We live in the tension between stability and change, trying to maintain a balance that has enough stability to be comfortable, secure, and reasonably predictable, and enough change to be interesting, challenging, and growth-enhancing.

In your life history writing you undoubtedly see the stable things, the things that have remained constant in your personality and in your life. You can also see how much you've changed in certain ways and how much your world has changed.

People Change As Time Passes

One way of looking at change is to look at a group of people who are roughly the same age. Sociologists call them cohorts, groups of people who were born around the same time. If you look at these people, say, as a high school graduating class, you can see how similar they are. They dress in a similar fashion, they listen to the same music, they've been educated in a similar manner, and they share many of the same values. What happens to the individuals in this graduating class as they grow older? They start careers, start families, move to other parts of the country, and experience many different things that affect their personalities and lifestyles. All these influences make the individuals in this graduating class become more and more different from one another. Psychologists would say they become more individuated, more unique as they grow older. In other words, rather than becoming more alike, people tend to become more different from each other as they grow older. This is especially true in today's world of fast-paced change and family mobility.

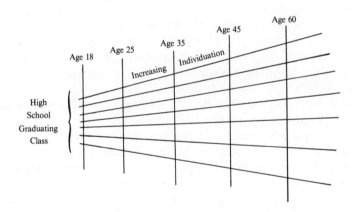

Looking at cohorts, or groups of people, is one way of looking at change. Another way of looking at change is to look at periods of change or transition in an individual's life. Is a person different at one age from who he was at an earlier age? There is much evidence to suggest that answer is "yes."

Jean Piaget, a pioneer in the field of child psychology, documents in his research how children think differently from one age to another.[11] For instance, if you take a tall skinny

47

drinking glass and a short fat one, and put five ounces of juice in each one, a very young child will tell you the tall glass has more.

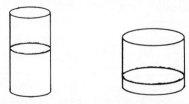

He actually sees the world through different eyes from those of an older child, who will recognize correctly that both glasses have the same amount—they're just different-shaped containers. In other words, children at different ages *see* and *think* differently.

Another psychologist, Robert Peck, describes a similar shift in thinking, from one age to another, for adults. It's not as simple as recognizing quantities, but it's a similar kind of reorientation toward the world, especially toward other people.

Peck says that four specific changes occur in a person's personality as he or she moves from youth into middle age:[14]

1. You begin to value wisdom more than you value physical powers. Insight and experience and good judgment become more important than physical strength or other qualities.

2. You begin to socialize rather than sexualize in your relationships with others. In other words, you stop thinking of people in terms of their beauty, physical attractiveness, and sexual potential, and you regard them more as other social beings with the possibilities of friendship and companionship.

3. You need to become emotionally flexible; that is, you need to be able to get emotional rewards from a number of different sources so that you aren't devastated when your children leave home or some other change occurs. If you don't develop this emotional flexibility, Peck says, you will become emotionally impoverished.

4. In a similar manner, you need to be mentally flexible, open to new ideas from the younger generation, open to the changes that keep happening in the world around you. If you do not develop this flexibility, you will become mentally rigid. We all know people who are like this—dead sure that there's only one right way to do things and it's *their* way! These people still cling to all the ideas and behaviors they were taught as children, and they are rigid and uncompromising. They resist change and new ideas at all costs.

According to Peck, the change doesn't stop in middle age. There are three more changes that people experience as they move into old age:

1. You need to have your ego (your sense of self) invested in a number of different activities and interests, so that you are not totally preoccupied with your work role. This is especially true for men, who define who they are almost completely in terms of what they do for a living. When retirement comes, they no longer have any sense of identity—they feel lost. Peck says that you should have a number of friendships, interests, and activities *outside* of work so that you can continue to have a healthy sense of self after you retire.

2. You must learn to transcend the limitations of your body or else you will become preoccupied with it. As old age brings some inevitable physical losses—strength, endurance, agility, vision, hearing, and memory all decline to a greater or lesser degree— you need to be able to transcend these physical things and maintain your outlook and spirit in old age. If you cannot rise above your physical problems, you will become preoccupied with them. We all have known some old people who have become so obsessed with their bodies and their failing health that they can talk of nothing else. Their world grows smaller and smaller until they have turned completely inward, and they constantly complain and worry about their arthritis, gout, rheumatism, poor digestion, etc.

3. Likewise, you must be able to transcend your own ego, your own mortal self, in order to see that the world will go on after you die. You must learn to see beyond your own finitude, to take an interest in posterity, in community, in the things you care about that will carry on after you are gone. Not to be able to transcend one's own life is to become preoccupied with it, to be filled with despair at its end.

It is clear, then, that there are some natural changes that occur as people grow older. There are physical changes, psychological changes, and spiritual changes. Most of these changes are incremental—they happen a little bit at a time, so that the changes are slow and gradual and we barely notice them at all.

Sudden Changes Come to Some

However, there are also changes that happen to a person very suddenly, often caused by some critical event. A severe illness or a close brush with death can change a person's personality and whole outlook on life. A marriage, a divorce, the birth of a child, the death of a loved one—all can bring about significant changes in a person. Any one of these can be a watershed event that changes the course of a person's development.

Religious experiences and conversions very often have this effect. The term "born again," used by many Christians today, indicates that the new person is radically different from his or her former self. Maybe you have undergone a conversion or had some other kind of religious experience. Think about all the ways it changed you as a person.

We make note of such changes in the people we know. We say "He's a changed man," or "She's not the person she was before." In many cases the change is a positive one, but not always. We may not be pleased with the changes that come about in our friends and family members. If the change is positive, we rejoice. If we think the change is negative, we may criticize, worry about, or avoid the person. We may complain that "I hardly know you anymore," or "You're not the same person I married."

Change in a person is sometimes brought about by something small or seemingly insignificant. It might be a book we read, or a small incident, or even an offhand comment. A very athletic man once told me how something he overheard had a huge impact on his self-image and his development. He was an overweight teenager with a low opinion of himself. One day he was in the locker room at school when he overheard one of the coaches say to another, "You know, that Vic is as strong as an ox!" The coaches didn't know he was around, since he was on the other side of the lockers. But that one comment, not intended for his ears, seared into his consciousness. He began to work very hard in P.E. classes and tried out for several sports. He lost weight, got in shape, and went on to a successful athletic career in college. He says that one little comment gave him the boost to his self-confidence that he needed. Someone else's faith in him gave him faith in himself.

So things that change your life can be subtle and gradual, or dramatic and immediate. They can be major events or small things. In thinking about your own life, can you recall any watershed events, any incidents that changed you as a person? You might want to devote a whole chapter in your life history to some critical event, some turning point in your life.

50

Change, then, is a natural part of the aging process. Changes occur as you mature, whether you like it or not. We are always changing, growing, evolving in many ways—socially, emotionally, spiritually, psychologically. Change can also occur because of specific events in your life, as we've just discussed. But what about *willful* change? What about changes that you *decide* to make in your life?

Choosing to Make Changes

Almost all of us have something about ourselves that we'd like to change. When we're thinking about changing ourselves, however, it's important to be clear about *what* we want to change. We need to draw a distinction between our *traits* and our *states.*

Your *states* are your moods, how you're feeling right now. You might be in a depressed state; you might be in a joyful state; you might be in an angry state. What do you do if you want to change the state you're in? People use lots of different methods to change their states. Often they do something physical, like jogging or going for a walk or a bike ride; maybe they listen to music or play a musical instrument. Maybe you're the kind of person who resorts to sleeping to change your mood, or maybe you eat to accomplish this. Many of us have specific "comfort foods" we eat to make ourselves feel better—chocolate is a favorite of many but certainly not the only comfort food available. Sometimes it is a special dish that your mother made for you or something your grandmother made.

Some people call up a friend when they need help changing a mood; others go to the movies or seek some other kind of escape. People of faith often turn to prayer or meditation or scripture reading. Some people reach for dangerous things, like drugs or alcohol, to change their moods. Other people take a walk on the beach or try to work out their troubles with pen and paper. Writing is very often an excellent way of dealing with negative states and working them out in a positive way.

What is evident in all these activities is the fact that states, or moods, are temporary conditions, always changing from day to day. They are also relatively easy to change.

Traits, on the other hand, are more permanent and much harder to change. Your traits are your personality characteristics. Maybe you're an optimist; maybe you're insecure; maybe you're an angry person. There's a big difference between being angry on occasion and being a basically angry person. If you're an angry person, it'll take a lot more than just a couple miles of jogging to change!

What do you do when you want to change a trait? Very often we turn to prayer. Haven't we all, at one time or another, prayed to God to help us change something about ourselves, some personality trait that we don't like? We ask God to make us less selfish and more generous; we pray to become more humble and less prideful; we try to be more patient, more loving, more Christlike.

Sometimes people seek therapy in an effort to change themselves. They have some personality trait that gets them into trouble or causes problems in their relationships with others, so they seek a therapist to help them change.

Other people try some form of self-discipline to change themselves. But whatever the method people choose, it is clear that it takes time, consistent effort, and discipline to change one's traits. It's not as simple as changing your state. If you are by nature a pessimist, it will take a tremendous amount of work over a long period of time to make your outlook more positive.

Can you change any trait you want to? How do you distinguish between the things you can change and the things you can't? Are there some things about yourself that you just have to learn to live with?

Some of this ties in with your beliefs about free will. Does free will give you the power to make conscious choices about your life, and do those choices also involve changing yourself? Or was your whole life determined by God before you were born, so you really can't change? It's a complex question for many Christians: free will vs. determinism. Different Christian traditions have different answers for the puzzle. It's an important issue to clarify for yourself before you begin trying to change yourself.

The Serenity Prayer gives a poetic answer:
> God,
> Grant me the serenity to accept the things I
> cannot change;
> Courage to change the things I can; and
> Wisdom to know the difference.

I have discussed this issue of how people change with my friends who are therapists. One told me that most people grow up in typically neurotic homes, but he felt that neuroses could be unlearned! Another therapist said that doing therapy is like dealing with a baby riding an elephant: the baby is the intellectual part of the person, and the elephant is the emotional. He said it's easy to change the baby, but it's a heck of a lot harder to try to move that elephant!

Albert Ellis, a leading figure in "rational-emotive" therapy, says that you can use your rational thinking to control and diminish the power of your emotions.[15] He says that we all carry around "tape recordings" in our heads, especially old tapes from our past. The problem, as Ellis sees it, is that people often play back old tapes from childhood that are no longer appropriate. What we need to do is stop playing those old tapes, which are usually negative, and replace them with new tapes, more positive tapes, which suit who we are as adults.

Roger Gould, who has written a marvelous book on life's changes called *Transformations,* has a similar idea.[16] He says we all have both a childhood consciousness and an adult consciousness. As one progresses through life, change is possible by increasing the dominance of the adult consciousness and decreasing our childhood consciousness. He developed a seven-step dialogue that one may carry on within oneself to aid in this process.

Different therapists take different approaches to change, but they all seem to agree that the possibilities for personal change are real, though not easy. Whether you seek a therapeutic approach to change, a self-discipline approach, or a spiritual approach, the desire is basically the same: to change your personality and your life so that you can be a better person, more like the ideal self that you carry around in your head.

How does life history help in this process? Writing your life history can help you clarify the dialectical tensions in your life, the polarities we mentioned earlier (privacy/community, masculine/feminine, young/old, stability/change, etc.) Through understanding tensions, you can make them easier to live with.

Writing your life history can also reveal areas of your life that you'd like to change. The potentials for change will make themselves apparent as your story unfolds.

And finally, by writing your life story and taking stock of the past, you will be in a better position to decide where you want to go in the future. You need to understand where you've been before you can know where you want to go.

Section II

Looking at Your Life

Everyone has a story to tell . . .
If only someone would listen,
If only someone would ask.

1

Your Life As a River

To describe something, metaphors are often better than mere adjectives. They are certainly more imaginative, more colorful, often even poetic. We talk about the "springtime of youth" or the "sunset years of later life." Both conjure up beautiful images in the mind. We often choose objects from the natural world to use as metaphors—animals, plants, seasons, minerals, etc. We can all understand and appreciate images drawn from nature.

To start writing your life story, describe your life as a river. Begin with the tributaries, the sources that fed your river in the beginning. Think about how your river grew larger as it progressed, with more sources feeding into it. The first sources are family; later sources might be friends, schoolteachers, ministers, neighbors, books, ideas, religious figures, political figures.

What kind of a river is your life? Is it slow and meandering? Is it quiet and deep? Is it fast and turbulent? Has it changed at different times in your life?

What sorts of obstacles has your river encountered? Did God put any boulders in your path? Did you flow around them, over them, under them? Was your river so strong that you pushed the boulder out of the way?

What have been the critical turning points in your life river? What were the turns you took? How would your life have been different if you had turned in another direction?

Who have you nourished with the river? Who has drunk from your life-giving waters? Children? Family? Friends? Strangers?

Getting married was an important turning point in my life. I met my wife in 1965 at John Burroughs Junior High; I was an English teacher, she, a student teacher. We met in April and were married in December. My marriage offered quite a contrast to that of my parents', which was an uncomfortable union of two incompatible people. I remember quite a few incidents, when I was quite young, of my parents' arguing and not getting along. Marriage presented an unpleasant picture to me until I was married myself. My wife and I are very compatible and have many of the same interests. Also, my father and mother were so immersed in their business that they had little time for me. This, I am sure, contributed to my poor performance in school before college. It was hard to call us a 'real family.' As a contrast my wife and I spend a lot of time with our son who was born in 1972. He does very well in school and is a very pleasant, congenial person. I learned how to be a parent by not following the example of my parents.

Exercise: *Metamorphosis*

Another metaphor you might try is that of metamorphosis. A caterpillar in youth, a cocoon at midlife, a butterfly in later life—is that you? Describe your own metamorphosis, your own evolution from one type of person to another dramatically different type.

Sometimes this is an accurate metaphor for people who have had a religious conversion or a spiritual awakening. They feel that they have become very different people. Other critical events can also dramatically change a person's life and personality. If this is true for you, write about your life as metamorphosis.

Exercise: *Chambered Nautilus*

For some people, particularly women, a seashell like the chambered nautilus is a particularly descriptive metaphor. The development is circular, with each stage being built on the foundation of preceding stages. The shell develops in an ever-widening spiral, and it does so in discrete stages.

Maybe the chambered nautilus fits the way your life has developed. Write about the stages and the widening spiral of your life.

Exercise: *My Life As a Tree*

Many other metaphors can be used to describe your life. Perhaps a tree is a good one for you, with roots, a trunk, and branches going off in different directions. The tree of life has flowers and bears fruit. Describe your life as a branching tree.

One woman told me that her life was more like crabgrass. It started with one plant, then sent out runners which would put down roots and develop into other plants. Her life was more like a hardy groundcover rather than a branching tree!

Whatever metaphor you choose, it will give you a good overview of your life, which will help you in writing about all the various aspects of your life in the coming chapters. Spend some time to get a general picture of your life's development.

2

Your Family

"There is no 'I' without 'we.' "[17]

Family is undoubtedly the most critical key to who we are. In the early years of childhood, our mother and father and other family members are our whole world. They care for us, feed us, and teach us how to walk and talk. They give us our earliest rules for living. Their influence on us is profound. Even without direct teaching, we pick up many behaviors and personality traits simply from being around them. By a kind of osmosis, we absorb much from the people we're around in those early formative years.

Our early family is the source of everything we need—food, warmth, protection, love, and communication. Such an important influence on us is naturally a major source of happiness to many people, as well as a source of pain to many others. Family is all-encompassing in the early years. If things are bad within the family, the effect on the child can be devastating emotional and psychological wounds that leave painful scars. How many people do we know who are still dealing with issues left over from childhood? Are you one of those people?

The family we have as adults is just as important as our family of childhood. Most people marry and have children. Some people who don't may create an adopted "family" of close friends. Some people participate only in a nuclear or immediate family. Others have an extended family with which they stay involved.

Think about your family, about the people with whom you grew up. What was the tone of your family? What did it feel like to be in your family? Was it warm? Loving? Noisy? Cool? Aloof? Quiet? Peaceful? Stimulating? Boring? Who reared you as a child? Your parents? Grandparents? Aunts or uncles? Step-parents? Foster family? Someone else? How did you feel about the people who reared you? What sort of relationship did you have with them? What was good about it? What was bad?

Who had the power in your family? How did you know? Who made the decisions? Who *thought* they made the decisions?

To whom did you go for comfort and love? To whom did you tell your secrets? To whom were you closest?

What were the things that drew your family close together? Hard times? Good times?

> The home that my parents purchased just prior to my birth was a leap of faith. It came precariously close to being lost in the Great Depression. It was at that time that my two maiden aunts came to live with us. These two aunts, Aunt Ernie and Elsie, were to contribute something very positive to my life during this period. Their care of me (and my mother during a time of sickness) and their contribution to the mortgage payments allowed our life to go on in spite of my Dad's loss of his job. They also brought a quiet piety that gently came alongside of my parents' faith expression. My Aunt Ernie thought God could hear her best if she prayed aloud. I can still hear her voice uttering in a muffled monotone her nightly prayers in German as I drifted off to sleep. I went through many years of my life knowing that I was named each night in those petitions which she earnestly offered to God. When the Depression eased, my aunts moved back to their own home, which had been rented out, and I got my bedroom back again. It felt good, but there was also something and somebody missing!

What were the things that tore your family apart?

What were some of the traditions that have been handed down through your family?

Who were the heroes in your family? Who were the rebels?

What were mealtimes like in your family? What were holidays like?

Did you have brothers or sisters? Were you close to them? Did you fight with them? What was your relationship like? How is your relationship with them today?

In what religious tradition were you reared? How did it influence your personality? What sorts of religious values were you taught? Have you continued in that religious tradition, or have you adopted another? Why?

What were you taught about God? What was your image of God? Did you pray when you were a child? What kinds of prayers? How has your prayer life changed as you grew up?

My earliest recollection of my beingness placed me in a loving, supportive home where mealtimes were the family meeting times, where setting a table always meant setting a place for one more than was already present. That place was for Elijah or an unexpected visitor. You see, I was born a black female into a family of black Jews. This was in the 1930s when black Jews for the most part were unheard of. It was a very difficult time for me because we lived in a black ghetto among Catholics, Protestants, other assortments of faiths, and those that did not subscribe to any faith. I remember clearly the Sabbath from Friday sundown to Saturday sundown, the time when Christian children could stay up late and visit or go to the movies. During this period I was not allowed to play even at home, we just sat around while my uncle, a rabbi, talked in a funny language with a hat too small for him sitting on the top of his head and a black and white shawl on with fringes on the end. In order to have any friends, I spent their religious day, Sunday, going to church with them. Consequently, in my formative years I had my share of religion by in-depth exposure to so many.

How did your childhood affect the way you raised your own children? Have you done things differently? What do you teach them about God? What values do you teach them?

Do your parents continue to have a significant influence on you today?

What would you like to change about your family? What would you like to preserve?

Were you loved? How did you know?

Exercise: *My Childhood Bedroom*

See if you can remember the bedroom you had as a child. What was it like? Can you draw a picture of it or a floor plan?

Was your bedroom an important place? Why or why not?

Did you share your room with anyone? A brother or sister? Someone else? How did sharing a room effect your relationship?

See if you can close your eyes and pretend you're back in your room. What does it feel like? Is it warm and safe? Is it crowded, with no privacy? Describe your feelings about being in your room. What are the sounds, the smells? What are the colors? The important objects?

Exercise: *A Photograph of My Family*

Pretend you're a photographer and you're going to take a family portrait of your own family. You want to arrange people in positions that symbolize their position in the family. Who would be in the center of the picture? (Who's the central figure in your family?) Who would be standing close to the person? Who would be on the outer edges of the picture? Would anyone be missing? Who's making funny faces at the camera, the family clown? Would anyone have their back to the camera? Why?

Which people in the picture would be touching each other? Who's smiling? Who's frowning? Why?

Try to sketch out what this family photograph would look like.

Exercise: *God and Family*

How does your earthly father affect your image of God the Father? Are they similar? Are they different? What do you think of when you think of "Father"?

What does the "Family of Man" mean to you? Do you feel like a family with other people?

How do you understand "children of God?" Do you feel like a child of God? Why or why not? What does it mean to be a child? Do you believe that all people are children of God? Are there people you know who don't seem like children of God? How do you feel about them?

What do the words "brother" and "sister" mean to you? In your family? In a religious sense?

3

The Role of Food in Your Life

For some people, food is simply a biological necessity. Food is fuel for the body—nothing more, nothing less. These people may even be annoyed at having to take time out from their activities to eat. They sometimes even forget to eat!

For many others, however, food plays a much more central role in life. They anticipate the next meal. They delight in the process of eating. Food for them is not simply fuel; it is much, much more.

While some people eat to live, others live to eat.

Food can be used for celebration. Food can be used for consolation. Food can be a reward. There are special holiday foods, such as turkey and pumpkin pie for Thanksgiving, cookies and baked treats for Christmas, candy at Easter. And there are foods associated with the seasons of the year. Have you ever noticed that you can't find eggnog at the market at any time of year except winter?

There are special foods that are "musts" on certain occasions—popcorn at the movies, hot dogs at ball games, cotton candy at the carnival, cake and ice cream for birthdays. These foods themselves take on heavy emotional significance.

Food can be used to alter moods. Chocolate is a favorite mood lifter for many people, but it is certainly not the only example.

And foods can have profound religious significance, such as bread and wine. When you "break bread" with others, no one would say you are *just eating,* for clearly there is much more going on than that.

What does food mean to you? What role does it play in your life? Is food important to you? Why or why not?

When you were a child, did anyone ever reward you with food, or console you with food? What kinds of food?

On the symbolic level food does represent memories and ideas. Chocolate reminds me of my grandparents who were loving and kind toward me and who usually prepared me the same dessert whenever I ate a meal at their house. The dessert was a candy bar, usually Suchard milk chocolate, broken up on orange Jello, covered with evaporated milk. I ate this concoction for years. If I eat a Suchard chocolate bar now-a-days, the very smell and taste of it conjure up memories of my grandparents; images of rooms where I played as a child are even brought back.

When you were ill, did someone make special foods for you? Did those foods make you feel better? Why?

What were your family's customs about food? Were mealtimes important occasions for the family?

Someone impressed upon me indelibly in my formative years that it was a sin to waste food. I still relive my pangs of conscience that I felt when I went behind a hedge to discard the dry crust from a jelly sandwich. That way God couldn't see me in my sin, but somehow I knew he did! Incredible! What a sophisticated concept I had of God in those days!

What role does food play in your life now?

Do you ever go on diets? Why? How do you feel about the diets? Do you feel deprived of pleasure? Do you feel good about the discipline?

Is it important to you whether food is homemade or storebought? Why?

Cooking has been a very positive element in my role as a homemaker. I like to prepare everything from scratch and everything fresh. It makes me happy to present a decent meal whether it is for my family or friends. Though I am not always wild about cooking, I find myself laboring with details to present a simple meal. I saw a sign somewhere which said the following: "Cooking is like sex— it should be entered into with abandon or not at all!"

Ready-made foods do not excite my spirit. In fact, it depresses me to open a can of food for consumption. It makes me feel unloved, and it does not nourish either my body or my spirit.

To share with someone else a special food I prepared is an expression of my love and this makes me happy.

Food symbolizes a blessing of God's endless flow of supply. It is sacred, and not to be wasted. It is a symbol of life.

What foods are connected to special occasions for you?

Do you use foods to alter your moods? How?

Is food a punishment or a reward?

How is food related to love?

What messages do you get about food from the culture in which you live?

What does TV tell you about food? Magazines, newspapers, advertising?

What role does food play in your social life?

Is food related to sex?

What is the relationship between food and your health? Your body image?

What role does food play in your family life? In your relationships with friends?

As I recall my childhood home, I vividly remember the preparation of food and its importance. It seems our kitchen was the center of all the activities. We had a large round table in the middle of the room, and I remember my mother leaning over the table laboring to create her special foods for our family, relatives, and friends, especially on Sunday. Sunday was a glorious day, filled with hustle and bustle, the smells of the kitchen, people coming and going, eating what my mother was preparing on her day off.

I was always stunned and bewildered by her endless and intense energy, devotion, and artistic abilities in preparing our foods. I always remember her telling us that preparing and sharing our food was an expression of love. So I grew up believing it.

Is food a symbol of other things for you?

Exercise: *"The Cookbook of My Life" or "This Is What We Ate When . . ."*

Another way of exploring the significance of food in your life is to make a cookbook. Take the recipes you have collected over the years and assemble them in a scrapbook or large notebook. On the same page with each recipe, write a personal story—something connected with that recipe. The story might be about an occasion when you prepared the recipe, or it might be a story about the person who gave you the recipe. Perhaps something funny or interesting happened once when you served that dish. If so, write about it.

This might turn out to be a very large project, but when you are finished you will have a wonderful book! It will be a collection of all your old recipes as well as an intimate personal account of an important aspect of your life. The cookbook would make a wonderful legacy to your children, grandchildren, and other family members. It could be a prized gift for friends. If you are artistic, you may want to include drawings or snapshots. You could photocopy several copies and put them in attractive binders.

However you treat the finished product, the exercise will reveal much intimate detail about the role food has played in your life.

Exercise: *"My Last Supper"*

If you were about to prepare a "last supper" for yourself, what foods would you serve? What would be the significance of each dish? Would you want to cook all the food yourself, or would you want other people to bring some of the dishes?

Who would you want to share your last supper with you? Why?

Exercise: *A Love Feast for God*

If you were in charge of preparing a love feast for God, what would you serve? Would you have food from different countries? Would you serve foods that have religious significance? Describe in detail the kind of feast you would prepare, who would attend, and where it would be held.

4

Your Life's Work

Life's work means different things to different people. For some, life's work is the way they earn a living; it is a career, an occupation. For others, it may be rearing children and making a home for the family. Life's work does not need to involve receiving money for services or labor; life's work is the primary activity in which one is productive. Your life's work is where you invest a significant portion of your time and energy. It is also very important in defining your identity.

Most people, when they take time to think about it, have more than one life's work. They may have had several careers during their lives, sometimes even simultaneously. For many Christians, their life's work is serving God, while at the same time they spend much time working as a teacher, a doctor, a housewife, an artist, etc. Perhaps it is helpful to think of a spiritual life's work and a secular life's work. For example:

As I grew older and entered parochial school I learned about vocations and avocations. One's vocation was one's calling from God. There were three vocations for human beings in God's schema—to married life, to single blessedness, and to the religious life. The tasks one performed, in whatever vocation one was called to, made up one's avocation. Or so I understood the teaching I heard from the nuns. So my dad was primarily a husband and father, my mother a wife and mother, and my aunt was single. Nuns and priests were in religion. Early on I decided I didn't ever want to be a nun, nor did my mom ever encourage me in that direction. I had no liking for single blessedness as exemplified by my unhappy, neurotic aunt. Clearly, marriage was to be my lot, providing I could find a husband, although it would be hard to find a man as wonderful as my dad. I didn't know any women who worked outside of the home. Somewhere along the line I learned about Madame Curie, who was wife and scientist, and the picture changed. Still, I saw her primary role as that of wife and mother. This point of view never changed.

In thinking about your own life's work, explore how your spiritual calling related to the work you did in the world. Were they two separate activities, or were they one in the same?

Did you maintain two or more life's works at the same time? Were you a wife and mother as well as a money-earner?

Is your life's work centered around your family? How have you been rewarded in this work?

How did you get into your major life's work? Did you choose it because your family expected it? Was it because of an influential teacher or some other role model in your life? When did you begin your life's work?

Was there any special training for your life's work?

What kinds of things were you interested in as a child? What did you want to be when you grew up? Why?

Did you feel that you had a special "calling" to your life's work? How did you know this? Have you been called to other kinds of work as well? How do you respond when you feel this calling?

How has your Christian faith affected your role as employer, employee, or coworker?

Who and what have been the biggest influences in the course of your life's work? People? Events? Books?

What have been the biggest challenges to you in your life work? Your biggest successes? Your biggest problems? Your worst failures?

How does your religion influence your ideas about "success" and "failure"?

If you have more than one life's work identity, which one has been the most important to you? Why?

What have you enjoyed the most about your life's work? What have you enjoyed least?

How much of your identity is invested in your life's work? If I asked you, "Who are you?" would you answer me by telling me about your work?

Exercise: *Men, Women and Work*

Many cultures, including our own, have certain definitions of what constitutes man's work and what constitutes woman's work.

This traditional division of labor is vividly depicted in the following excerpt from a sixty-year-old life history student:

As a young child I had a strong sense of the difference in the way men and women seemed to have their lives organized. There was a clear pattern in the life of our family. Each weekday morning my father, dressed in sartorial splendor, crisp and clean and smelling wonderful, would march off down the street to some mysterious place called "work." My mother stayed home to cook and clean and, it seemed to me, spend hours in our basement leaning over a huge sink scrubbing clothes. In summer the clothes were hung on lines out in the backyard, in winter on lines in the warm basement near the furnace. She also made beds, cleaned and dusted the house, picked clothes off the floor, washed windows every so often, polished silver, and shopped daily. It seemed to me that she never stopped performing household tasks and she appeared very tired in the evening. Even so she would spruce up every evening just before Dad would appear trudging up the street not quite so jauntily as he had left in the morning. He too appeared tired, but I was unaware of his activities, although it was apparent that his did not take such a toll on his clothing as did my mother's on hers. Her "housedress" was dirty at the end of the day and she always changed into a prettier one before my dad arrived.

. . . So I thought women stayed home and men went to "work."

Does this description fit your experience of men's work and women's work? Has your experience been different? How?

Do you think there should be differences in men's work and women's work? Or should they be the same?

Do you think the cultural definitions of work have changed? What makes you think so?

What does the Bible say about work for women and work for men? Do you agree? Why or why not?

How do your religious values affect your ideas about men, women, and work?

Exercise: *"My Life's Work Would Have Been Different If. . . "*

Many people have unfulfilled desires concerning the life's work they hoped for; they had to change plans due to money problems, early marriage, a death in the family, or other unanticipated events. Are you one of those people? How would your life's work have been different if events had happened differently?

What would you go back and change about your life's work, if you could?

How would this have changed the rest of your life? Do you think you would have been more fulfilled, happier?

Exercise: *My Life's Work in the Future*

What will be your life's work from here on out?

Do you plan to make any changes in your life's work? What are they?

Do you feel a calling to do something different, or are you meeting your calling now?

5

The Role of Money in Your Life

Money is one of the most important themes in people's lives. It is a necessity of life; it can be an obsession or a preoccupation; it can be a burden. We all deal with money on a daily basis, and its effect on our lives is profound. Money is much more than just a means of exchange. Money is a symbol of many other things: power, status, love, sex, self-esteem, personal worth, control, security, etc. For some people, money is a devil; for others, money is God's way of rewarding the righteous.

What has been the role of money in your life? Describe both the negative and positive aspects of money in your life.

What were you taught about money when you were a child? How was money treated in your family? Were you poor or well-off? How did this affect your lifestyle?

> The noise in the hallway was not familiar to me. As I lay in my bed the voices became more and more strained. I quietly got out of bed and opened the door to see some strange men taking my stepfather out on a stretcher. I was told to go back to bed—that everything would be all right. But it wasn't. That night he died, and within one month my life changed drastically. When he died, unknown to my mother, he left us with many debts which had to be paid. The most pressing one was the Federal Government—he had not paid income taxes for years. And so we lost the main home in Tampa, our cars, boat, and were left with only the bare essentials for furniture. We moved into our two-bedroom beach house on Redington Beach. Thus, at age eleven, I became very aware of the importance of making money, saving money, and being responsible for debts you incur.

Who earned the money in your family? Who controlled the way it was spent? Was money a problem or an issue of conflict in your family?

Was there any connection between religious values and the way money was handled in your family?

How important is money to you now? Why? Have your attitudes about money changed as you've gotten older?

Do you tithe to your church? Why or why not?

Do you give money to charities? Why or why not?

What is the relationship between God and money, in your opinion?

Do you think there is any relationship between money and love? Explain your experiences in this regard.

Does money affect your self-esteem? How?

Do you worry about money, or the lack of it? How much do you think about money?

How do you react to people who have lots of money? Do you have any "rich relations" in your family? How are they regarded in the family?

What was the first time you earned any money? How did you feel about it? How did it affect your later ideas about money?

What have been your greatest financial successes? Your biggest financial mistakes?

Do you consider yourself a stingy person? A frugal person? A generous person? A spendthrift? Why?

Do you ever give money away? How do you feel about it?

Have you ever had to ask for money or borrow money? How did you feel about it?

Exercise: *"If I Had a Million Dollars . . ."*

Children often fantasize about having lots of money, and they share stories with each other about what they would do and buy if they had a huge amount of money. Try to put yourself into that mode of fantasy. What would you do, today, if you had a million dollars? Would you change your lifestyle? How? What would you buy first? Would you give any money away? Would there be any negative aspects to being wealthy? Is it fun to be wealthy?

Exercise: *Money and Work*

What is the connection between money and your life's work? Is money the most important reason why you work? What are the other reasons for your life's work? Would you continue to work if you were rich and didn't have to work? Why or why not? Would you change your life's work if you were rich?

6

Your Heroes

Heroes are the people whom we admire and often try to imitate. Heroes personify the ideals in which we believe and exemplify the kinds of characteristics we would like to have. Heroes are respected and even loved. Heroes inspire people to follow them, often with great loyalty.

Heroes can be real or mythical; they can be historical figures or people who are living today. They may be heroes to large numbers of followers, or they may simply be a personal hero—someone you admire and try to emulate.

Who have been the heroes of your life?

Who was your earliest hero? Did you ever try to imitate your hero? How? Did you ever actually meet your hero, or was it someone you admired from afar?

Have you had a series of heroes? Are they all the same type of figure, or are they very different from each other? What does this reveal about your aspirations and your ideas about yourself?

Where did your heroes come from? Did you find them in the Bible? Did you learn about them in Sunday school? Was your minister ever a hero to you? Was Moses a hero? Abraham? Jesus? Peter? Paul? Mary? Sarah? Esther? Any other biblical figures? How did your religious training and beliefs influence your choice of heroes?

Were there heroic figures in your family? Who were they? Why were they heroes? Are they still heroes today? How did they influence your life?

I didn't realize it at the time, but I guess the feeling that I had for my father was more hero than daddy.

In an environment filled with poverty, superstition, crime and wasted minds, my father was the antithesis. He was always clean—by that I mean dressed well, had the latest car, always a Cadillac; he even wore spats over his shoes. He did not live at home; he always came calling with gifts for me and the other kids. He never yelled or hit me. He was an ideal father. He was my hero. After all, isn't a hero someone you look up to, someone that stands out from a crowd, someone that rises above the everyday mundane circumstances? And you can bet just how hard I tried to imitate him. I loved dancing like my father—and I was very good at it. I yearned for the glitter and glamor of the stage, the night life and all that went with it. I strived so to be like my hero—to live without want, to have my needs met, to have others look up to me.

Did you ever have TV or movie heroes? Who were they? How did they shape your ideas about the kind of person you wanted to be?

Have you ever had any political heroes? Who? Why? What sorts of characteristics did they exemplify?

What about literary heroes? What books have shaped your life? What autobiography that you've read had the biggest impact on your life? How?

What does it mean to be a hero? How far do you go in following your hero?

Have you ever been disillusioned with your heroes? What happened?

Are your heroes allowed to be human? What if they let you down? Are they still your heroes?

Have you ever been a hero to someone else? What was it like? Did you enjoy it? What are the responsibilities of being a hero to someone?

Do you think it's good or bad to have heroes? What happens if it's carried too far? Have you ever gone too far with your heroes?

When I think of the word "hero/heroine," I consider persons that I admire. Persons who have qualities that I want to develop in myself. The expression "hero *worship*" doesn't really apply in my life because I can't fathom "worshipping" someone—a human being. I worship *God*. Losing my head over a celebrity or going bonkers as I've witnessed others over Elvis, for example, has always been astounding to me, and I've watched in disbelief.

Who are your heroes now? Why? How do they help you? What sorts of images come to mind when you think of your heroes?

Exercise: *My Ideal Hero*

Make a list of all the qualities you think your hero should have. In other words, construct a checklist of all the characteristics someone must have to qualify as your personal hero. This might be a composite of all the heroes you've had in your life, or maybe you just make up these qualities out of your own imagination.

Try to be as complete as possible. Include physical characteristics as well as personality traits. Does it matter to you what your hero looks like? Is your hero male or female? Does your hero have any negative qualities? Could you draw a picture of your hero?

Exercise: *Jesus As Hero*

Think about Jesus as your hero. What qualities does he have that you admire? Make a list of the things that make Jesus a hero.

Is Jesus perfect?

Does Jesus have any weaknesses or negative characteristics?

Is Jesus your hero? Do you try to emulate him in your daily life? Do you try to cultivate his qualities in yourself? Do you strive to be Christlike?

What happens when you don't measure up? When you set a perfect standard, like Jesus, how do you feel when your own actions are less than perfect?

Does having Jesus as a hero help and inspire you? Or does it disappoint and frustrate you? Or both?

Exercise: *"If I Were in Charge of TV . . ."*

Many people today complain about television and the terrible role models that are presented for young people. Sometimes the heroes are antiheroes, and youngsters try to copy them in real life.

If you were in charge of television—if you were the script-writer and director, what kinds of heroes would you put on TV? What kinds of stories would you write?

Try writing a two- or three-page story outline describing the hero or heroes and what they would be doing in the show.

Do you think other people would like your show? How would your heroes be different from other TV heroes today?

7

Your Health History and/or Your Body Image

Your body is your physical presence in the world. Your mind and your soul both reside within your body, and the three aspects of yourself—body, mind, soul—live in intimate relationship to each other. Holistic health science has taught us about caring for all three aspects of the self in order to maintain complete health. One cannot try to heal the body without dealing with the mind and soul, too; and vice versa.

Your "body image" has to do with how you perceive your own body, how you think and what you feel about it. Some people like their bodies, while others think their bodies are ugly.

How well do you get along with your body? Do you like it? Do you dislike it? Why or why not?

Do you have a fat self-image? Do you always think you're overweight, even when you're not?

Do you think you're too skinny? Too short? Too tall?

What part of your body do you like the best? What part do you like the least? What would you like to change about your body if you could?

Is your body a temple? How do you treat it? Do you abuse it? Do you treat it carefully?

Do you feel that your body is a gift from God? Has God blessed you in any physical ways? What are your physical treasures? Pretty eyes, soft skin, wonderful hair, dexterous hands, nimble feet, powerful muscles, etc?

How did you feel about your body when you were growing up? How did you feel in relation to other people? Was it painful? Did you feel OK? Did you ever wish to have a different kind of body? Why?

How has your health been during your life?

Were you a sickly child or a robust child? How were you treated? How did this affect your personality?

In grade school I was labeled "underweight" but was not sickly or hampered in any activities. Significant sicknesses or injuries during my boyhood (besides the usual childhood cycle of measles, mumps, chicken pox, and whooping cough) included a broken left wrist. My urban awkwardness manifested itself in a headlong fall from a loaded haywagon, which occured when I failed to hear the hoarsely-uttered command to the horses given by my grandfather. Because I am left-handed, the cast which I had to wear for some weeks significantly altered my body-world. As a result of this accident, however, I am increasingly ambidextrous.

What are the illnesses you've had in your life? Disabilities? Handicaps? Do you think you were afflicted with them for a reason? How did your faith help you in dealing with illness, disability, and pain? Have you found meaning in your physical suffering? How?

What have pain and illness taught you about yourself?

How do you behave when you're sick? Are you a stoic? Do you want to be babied and pampered? Do you want to be left alone? Do you become grouchy?

How do you take care of your health?

What is the relationship between your *physical* and *spiritual* health?

In retrospect, I wish I had been more disciplined in my exercise and eating habits in the earlier years of my professional life. A more operational "theology of the body" would have resulted in my having been a more responsible caretaker of my body, that unique and indispensable dimension of my being-in-the-world.

Exercise: *My Body As a Car. . .*

Describe your body as a car. What kind of a car is it? What make and model is it? Is it a foreign car or domestic? Is it full-size or compact? Is it a luxury car? Is it a sedan or a sports model?

Does your car perform well? Is it reliable? Does it start easily in the morning? Does it handle well?

What kinds of maintenance problems do you have? Do you get regular checkups and tuneups?

Has your car had any major accidents or breakdowns?

What kind of fuel do you put in your car?

Is your car a newer model or an older model? Would you call your car a classic?

Does the car need body work, or is it in pretty good shape?

8

Your Sexual Development and Your Changing Sex Roles

God created human beings male and female. Your identity as male or female affects every aspect of your life. You are labeled according to gender the minute you are born, and the world treats you differently according to that label. Different cultures have different ideas about what it means to be male or female. What ideas did you grow up with?

When did you first learn that boys and girls are different? How did you feel about it?

> My recognition of my feminine identity came from language (I was called a girl); from early recognition that my anatomy was different from that of my three brothers; from the difference in the way I was handled (much more gently than the rough-and-tumble play with my brothers); from the anxious solicitude with which my mother tracked me down when I was out of her view for too long. My brothers zipped off on their bikes early on, disappearing for hours, whereas I was much more accountable for my whereabouts. Somehow the world seemed to contain more dangers for me that it did for my brothers, so I was more carefully guarded. I wore enormous bows in my short hair and lovely smocked dresses. My toys were different from the boys' toys, though frequently not acceptable to me. I constantly received dolls as presents but rarely played with them except as victims or patients. My dad was much softer and gentler with me than with my brothers, with whom he rough-housed. Somehow girlness was conveyed to me in a multiplicity of ways and I had mixed feelings about this identity as I matured.

What were the toys you enjoyed and the games you played as a child? Were some toys or games inappropriate because they were for the opposite sex? How did you feel about that?

What sorts of clothes did you wear as a child? How did these affect your thinking about yourself as a boy or girl?

Were you overly protected? Did you have a lot of freedom? Was it because you were a girl or a boy?

How did you handle your emotions? Was it OK to cry? Was it OK to become angry? Was it OK to fight? Were emotions supposed to be handled differently by boys and girls?

People mature at different rates in terms of sexual development. Puberty can be a source of pride or a source of shame. What was it for you? How did you feel about the changes in your body? How did you deal with sexual urges?

Was sex confusing for you? Mysterious? Dirty? Sacred? Natural? Special?

How did you get your sex education? Parents? Friends? Brothers or sisters? Books? Movies or TV? Religious training?

How has your Christian faith influenced your ideas about sex? Do you refer to the Bible for guidance in this area?

How do you feel about your sexuality? How have your ideas changed during your life? Has your sexual behavior changed?

Feminine identity in a Catholic culture had two faces— the sacred and the profane. We were daughters of Eve, and original corruptor of gullible man, yet inheritors of the compliant nature of Mary, whose most famous statement was "Be it done unto me according to thy word." The Eve was part and parcel of all women, inherent in our sexual power over men, yet, the real intent of God the Father's creation of a second human being from Adam's rib was to provide a helpmate, an assuager of loneliness, an ancillary figure to spiff up life even in Paradise. But we destroyed man's life in Paradise by our friendship with snakes and, as a result, we were cursed to bear children in pain and travail. I don't know how they would have come forth had Paradise not been lost.

I learned to love and depend on the Blessed Virgin in spite of her biblical formlessness. Her personality, other than her docility, is not very well delineated in the New Testament. But the amount of myth about her in Christian tradition is inestimable. Even as I write now I have some sense of misgiving as if I am writing sacrilege, a word that still sends a chill down my spine. The myths became part of my belief system, and Mary became my patron and protector the more I was exposed to those myths. She was very real to me, and I struggled hard to acquire the gentle and giving qualities attributed to her and to quell the aggressive tendencies that sometimes seemed part of my nature. I never thought of those tendencies as masculine; rather, they had aspects of the profane. I really did want to be a saint when I was a child. I felt that a saint fulfilled the nature that God had designed for him or her, and I wanted to do that.

How does your faith guide your ideas and behavior as a wife, mother, sister, daughter?

How does your faith guide your ideas and behavior as a husband, father, brother, son?

What does it mean to be a man?

What does it mean to be a woman?

What is the ideal relationship between man and woman?

Exercise: *Advice to the Next Generation*

Much has been written in the past twenty-five years about the "battle of the sexes" and "women's liberation" and "men's liberation." Given all that you have personally experienced and witnessed in social changes and sex role expectations, what advice would you give the next generation concerning male/female relationships? See if you can come up with a list of five or ten guidelines in dealing with the opposite sex. Your list can be humorous or serious or both—whatever seems appropriate to you.

Exercise: *Meditations on Growing Up Female or Meditations on Growing Up Male*

Poetry has a long history of association with love and sex. Write a brief poem (or a longer one if you like) about what it has been like for you to grow up as a sexual creature. Maybe your poem will rhyme; maybe it won't. Try to use the poetic to capture your own private experiences in this sensitive area of life.

Exercise: *"If I Had Been Born the Opposite Sex. . ."*

Did you ever want to be the opposite sex? How would your life have been different? Describe how you imagine your life would have been if you'd been born the opposite sex. How would you have been treated differently? Would your education and training have been different? What career options would have been different?

Do you think your life would have been better or worse?

9

Your Experiences with Death

Death comes into your life at both expected and unexpected times, affecting your life in many ways. You may have lost a beloved pet when you were a child; you may have experienced the loss of parents, grandparents, dear friends, a spouse, children, a brother, or a sister. Perhaps the death of a political hero or a religious leader affected you profoundly.

How have your experiences with death affected your life and your personality? How have the experiences with death been different from each other? Have your reactions to death changed over the years? Have your ideas concerning your own death changed?

What does your Christian faith tell you about death? Have the Christian teachings helped you in coping with the death of loved ones? How?

How did you feel about death when you were a child?

My father died when I was four. I was in the kitchen with my mother when we heard him fall, all the way down from upstairs head over heels, thump. Time stopped. A moment of putting who and what together without why. Then I stopped. Amnesia. Everything happened, nothing happened. What's the difference? Did someone scream, what do their faces say? I can only lead my memory from the empty stairs to the pale blue pajamas at this leg; it won't reach past the plaid edge of his bathrobe. One fixed scene, a photograph: his head will not be in it. Just the blood. Later my mother was talking on the phone by the grey armchair. I stood off at a distance, helpless. I'm sure the event must have terrified me absolutely, for I can still feel the numbness, and isolation.[19]

When did you go to your first funeral? How did you react?

How was death talked about and treated in your family? How did you understand it? Did it frighten you? Confuse you?

Have you ever been so sick you thought you might die?

Have you had any other close brushes with death? What were they? How did you feel about them? How do you feel now?

What effect did the threat of death in wartime have on you? Were you fearful for loved ones? For yourself?

Have you ever killed anyone? How did you feel about it?

> Stone dead, he was. Eyes wide open, staring at nothing. A thin veneer of blood curling at the corner of his lips. Two gaping holes in his chest. Right leg half gone. My first combat fatality. Violent death had raped me and usurped my virginity. A lifeless corpse where only moments before a heart beat its customary seventy pumps in one orbit of the second hand. It is one thing to hear about death; it is quite another to watch it happen. I went over to the nearest tree and vomited my guts out.[20]

Do you feel guilty about anyone's death? Helpless? Angry? Resentful? Relieved? Abandoned? Joyful? Have you ever felt responsible for anyone's death, even though you didn't cause it? How did it affect your life?

How do you feel about your own death? What kind of a death would you like to have?

Have you ever thought about or attempted suicide? Why? How do you feel about it now?

Is death an enemy or a friend for you?

Exercise: *Unfinished Business*

Do you have any unfinished business with friends or relatives that you would like to settle before you die? Anyone to whom you'd like to say "I Love You" or "I'm sorry" or "Please forgive me" or "I forgive you"? Too often in life we leave important things unsaid until it's too late. We let old grudges smolder until it's too late to forgive or be forgiven. Through our stubbornness and pride, we miss opportunities for reconcilation and peace.

If you knew you were going to die very soon, what unfinished business would you want to take care of? Who would you call? Who would you want to see? What would you say?

Exercise: *My Obituary*

Write your own obituary as you would like it to be if you died today. What do you want people to remember most about you? What is your most important achievement in life to date? Family? Career? What are your best qualities? What were the especially interesting or unusual aspects of your life and personality? Is there a favorite picture you'd like printed with your obituary?

10

The Loves of Your Life

Love, according to the song, "makes the world go 'round." Love inspires art and poetry and great acts of heroism. Love is the basis for all the great religions of the world. Love is personal and private; love is social and public. Love is something that *everyone* wants and needs.

Without love, a baby withers and dies in a condition called marasmus. Without love, the grieving spouse dies soon after his beloved wife. Without love, we are filled with loneliness, anxiety, despair, and hopelessness. Human beings need love just as much as they need air to breathe, water to drink, and food to eat. Without love we are emotionally hungry; if deprived too long, we grow starved and desperate. Don't we all know someone who is emotionally starved and desperate for love? Have you ever been that someone?

What and who have been the loves of your life?

It took a long time for me to admit, even to myself, that I did not have a happy, storybook childhood. Fortunately, along with that acknowledgement comes the revelation that few people did.

Perhaps until the age of six my life was happy and normal. I don't seem to recall any hidden traumas during that period, but at that point in order to make ends meet, my mother went to work. Her "temporary" job which started at my sixth year didn't end until after my marriage and the birth of my first son!

Throughout my childhood my wish in blowing out each candle on my birthday cakes was that "Mommie can quit work." I really did miss having my mother at home with me, doing the things for me and with me that my friends shared with their mothers.

Can you remember your earliest awareness of love? What was it like? What were the circumstances? Who or what was the object of your love?

81

In what forms did you receive love as a child? Who made you feel loved? How?

How did your loves change as you grew older? Were your loves primarily people? What about places, objects, or ideas? Did you love any of these?

How has love disappointed you in your life? How did the disappointment affect later loves?

How have your various loves shaped your personality and life?

My life like many others' lives has been and is a search for love. My definition of love is acceptance and appreciation. Self-love must be part of a life—self-acceptance and self-appreciation. Strangely, that is a love that is very elusive; often late in arriving. Sometimes, it never comes.

How much simpler it would be to begin as a child with such a positive concept that we automatically love ourselves and feel worthy. No one to put us down; no one to make us feel guilty; no one to deprecate our efforts. What a wellspring to give from! Love is the only emotion I know that multiplies as it is used. All the others dissipate and weaken. Love grows stronger.

How have your ideas about love changed throughout your life?

How is Christian love different from other kinds of love (or is it)?

Who loves you now? How do you know?

How do you know God loves you? How do you respond to God's love?

Exercise: *Definition of Love*

Richard Burton once defined love as "a very large degree of tolerance." How do you define love?

Write a sentence or a paragraph giving your definition of love.

Exercise: *What Does Love Look Like?*

Draw or paint a picture of love. You can use figures, colors, symbols, etc. Your only limit is your imagination.

Exercise: *"How Do I Love Thee? Let me count the ways . . . "*

We express our love in many, many different forms. Choose someone special in your life, and make a list of all the ways you love him or her.

Exercise: *"Love Is a Many Splendored Thing"*

We use the word "love" in many different ways, to express different but related feelings. That is to say, there are lots of kinds of love—spiritual love, agape, brotherly love, filial love, romantic love, sexual love, aesthetic love, etc.

Make a list of all the different kinds of love you can think of. Share your list with a friend or a family member, and see if they can think of other kinds of love you may have missed. What does the length of your list tell you about the importance of love in your life?

11

The Hates of Your Life

"For everything there is a season, and a time for every
matter under heaven: a time to be born, and a time to die; . .
. a time to embrace, and a time to refrain from embracing . .
. a time to love, and a time to hate . . ."
—Ecclesiastes 3:1,2,5,8.

Hate is something that most people don't want to acknowledge or talk about. It is a forbidden emotion, especially for the
devout Christian. But hatred is a fact of life. Religious hatred has
fueled holy wars for thousands of years. Hatred is in evidence
everywhere we look.

In our personal lives, hate can exert just as strong an influence
on our lives as love can. A man who grows up hating his father
and vowing to be just the opposite kind of man is still as
controlled by his father as the man who loves his. The hate we
feel for people or for things has a powerful effect on the way our
lives develop.

If indeed there is "a time to love, and a time to hate," then we
should spend some time reflecting on our hates, just as we have
reflected on our loves.

Is hate the opposite of love? Or is it closely related to love?

What sorts of people, things, ideas, places have you hated?
How has it affected your life?

When was the first time you hated someone or something?
What did it feel like?

When you were growing up, what were you taught about
hate? How have your ideas changed?

Is it OK to hate? Is it a sin? Why or why not?

What does the Bible teach you about hate?

Do you demonstrate your hatred or do you keep it inside?

Have you ever hated someone so much you wanted him to die?

Have you ever hated someone whom you also loved? What is it like to have a love/hate relationship? How do you deal with it?

Exercise: *Hate Is . . .*

Hate is harder to describe than love, for most people. Write out your definition of hate in a couple sentences or a paragraph. Think about what it really means when you say you hate something.

Exercise: *The Things I Hate . . .*

Make a list of all the things in life you hate. These can be people, places, objects, ideas, principles, institutions, attitudes, etc. Be as complete as possible. You don't have to share your list with anyone, so feel free to add to your list.

When you are finished, write one sentence for each item describing *why* you hate it, or him, or her. Do you feel different *kinds* of hatred, just as you feel different kinds of love?

Exercise: *Hate in Action*

Just as love inspires us to take action, so does hate. What do you *do* about the people or things you hate? Do you feel it's OK to express your hatred, or should you bottle it up inside? What are the consequences?

What do you intend to do about the things you listed on your hate list? Why?

12

Your Moral Development

Moral development is a critical aspect of all our lives, yet it is often a difficult subject to talk about since it is hard to define the word "moral." We use the word all the time, and we all seem to have an understanding of what "moral" means. Is one's choice of food a moral issue? Is one's choice of art or music a moral issue? Is paying taxes a moral issue? Is wearing underwear a moral issue? You can get into endless debates on these questions because people define morality so differently and because standards of morality change over time.

In general, ethicists define a moral issue as one which has a significant impact on other people. This does not help cut down the amount of debate, since one can argue that almost *everything* has a significant impact on others, either directly or indirectly.

Moral issues have to do with our ideas about right and wrong, or good and bad. Right and wrong have to do with *actions;* good and bad have to do with *people* or *things.* How you define good and bad, right and wrong, is a result of early childhood training, cultural norms, the legal system, your religious training and beliefs, and many other factors.

How have you evolved as a moral person? What are your ideas about right and wrong actions? What for you constitutes a good person? How have these ideas changed throughout your life?

Who first taught you right from wrong? Can you remember an early childhood incident when you were caught doing something that was wrong? How were you punished? Who was the authority? What were the *reasons* used for telling you that something was wrong? How do you feel about that incident today?

My morality was crystalized for me in tenth grade. I had cheated on a chemistry exam—a friend had graded it and changed the answers for me. It wasn't even an exam, just a quiz. I don't know why, but I felt I had done something very wrong. I had only gotten a C in chemistry the first quarter—this from a straight-A student, so I guess I was desperate. But it still felt wrong. After class I went up to Mr. Parker and told him I'd not gotten the grade he had in his book but had actually missed more questions. I'll never forget his reply: "Well, I can certainly give you an A for something besides correct answers." I was stunned. Honesty felt good and it was being rewarded. I never cheated again and had utter contempt for all those in college who did. Being a pre-med major, I saw cheaters proliferate in each class.

Who was the primary person who did most of your moral teaching? Your mother? Your father? Someone else? What sorts of ideas did they teach you about what it means to be a "good person"? Who was considered to be a good person in your family, or in the community? Why?

As a child, did you look at the world as black and white? Good and bad? Was everything either good or bad? Were there any gray areas—things that could be good or bad, depending on the circumstances? How did you decide what was good and what was bad in relation to these circumstances?

What role did religion play in your moral development? Was hell invoked as the ultimate punishment? Did anyone ever threaten that God would punish you for doing certain things? Which things? How did you *feel* about this?

What were you taught about sin? Which things were sins and which ones weren't? How did you atone for your sins? What role did Jesus play?

What was your image of God? Was he stern? Were you afraid of him? Was he warm, loving, and forgiving? How did you know you were forgiven?

Can you be a moral person without being a religious person? How?

Can you be a religious person without being a moral person? How?

In other words, how does your religious faith influence your behavior and your definition of certain things as moral issues?

To me, the worst sin is being indifferent to the suffering of others, to the torture of animals and to the destruction of our environment. This sin is creating a hell on earth of mutual destruction. The answer to this is to be *moral,* to care and to act, for the good of us all.

Can you compose a definition of what is a moral issue for you? Have your ideas about this changed? Does something that you once considered a moral issue no longer fit into that category?

Who or what has influenced you at various times in your life to change your ideas about morality? A person, a book, a teacher, an idea or a principle, a certain experience or incident? How has your behavior changed?

How do you teach your children about right and wrong, good and bad? If you don't have any children, how would you like other people to teach their children about morality? Or how might you teach your own in the future?

Exercise: *My Moral Identity*

There are a number of ways to conceptualize your moral identity, and using diagrams can be helpful to clarify your ideas.

One way to think about your identity is to regard it as a pie, with different segments:

Depending on your personality, the segments can be equal in size or all different in size.

Your identity has lots of different segments, and your moral identity is simply one aspect of your overall identity.

Another way of thinking about your identity is to use the

metaphor of an onion to describe yourself. Your identity then would be in layers, looking something like this:

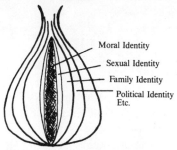

Moral Identity

Sexual Identity

Family Identity

Political Identity
Etc.

In this concept, your moral identity forms the *core* of your character; it is the foundation upon which all other aspects of your identity are built. It gives the shape and contours to your total identity.

Which of these two diagrams best captures your own moral identity? If neither one seems very accurate to you, can you think of another way to diagram your moral identity? Try your own concept on a sheet of paper and write a brief explanation.

Exercise: *Images of God*

What metaphors do you use when you think about God? What metaphors best capture the qualities of God?

How is God your Father? What qualities do you associate with God as Father?

Is God a policeman? Does he enforce rules, punish people, protect people? Explain how.

Is God like a shepherd—tending the flock, carrying the lamb over his shoulders? How is God a shepherd?

Are there other metaphors which you would use to express the qualities of God? Write a paragraph on each metaphor you choose.

Exercise: *Moral Influences*

Briefly describe how the following people or things were influences in your moral development:

—parents
—other family members
—religion and church
—teachers

—TV, movies, and radio
—books, newspapers, magazines
—friends
—other influences

89

13

Time

Time is a universal experience; it is a fundamental aspect of life for all human beings. Time may be measured chronologically, in minutes, hours, days, and years, or it may be measured emotionally, in heartbeats, tears, laughter, love, and memories.

God is timeless, but human beings are time-bound. We kill time, waste time, make time, lose time, mark time, spend time, and have a good time. Time is the foundation of our lives.

Our awareness of time changes as we grow older. For an anxious child, an hour can seem an eternity. For an adolescent, time and the good times fly by quickly. For the young adult moving up the career ladder, there never seems to be enough time. For the middle-aged person, there is an increasing awareness that one's allotted time is limited. For the old, time is sometimes a gift, sometimes a burden. Our experience of time varies throughout our lives.

How do you think about time? Are you conscious of time, or is it something you take for granted?

Do you think of time as a friend or as an enemy? Do you ever try to control time? How?

How did you feel about time when you were a child? What was time like when you were in school? What was time like when you were on vacation, as in summer? What was time like on holidays? What was time like in church?

How did your experience of time change as you got older?

What's your attitude toward time now? Do you worry about time?

What's the relationship between time and money in your life? Do you invest both your time and your money carefully? Are you generous with your time and money? Are you careless with your time and money?

Do you often waste time?

Do you prioritize how you will spend your time?

Are you a punctual person, or are you always late for things? How does this relate to your ideas about time?

Has any particular experience or incident in your life changed your attitude about time? How did this happen?

Do your religious values affect the way you deal with time? How?

Exercise: *My Life As a Clock*

Draw a clock face:

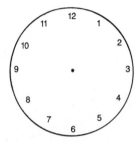

If your life is twelve hours long, what time is it now in your life?

How much time has gone by? How much time do you have left? How do you feel about this time in your life?

Exercise: *In the Rest of My Life . . .*

Make a list of the ten most important things you want to accomplish or do during the rest of your life. Describe why each of these ten things is important to you.

Exercise: *How I Spend My Time . . .*

List your favorite twenty things you enjoy doing. How many of them have you done in the past month? What does this tell you about how you allocate your time and energy? Are you really spending time on things that are important to you ? Are you spending your time on things you enjoy?

Try making a time budget just like you make a financial budget. Allocate a certain percentage of your daily or weekly time to each activity. See how well you can stick to your budget and maintain your priorities for your time.

14

The Meaning of Your Life

"Me"

Born screaming small into this world—
Living I am
Occupational therapy twixt birth and death—
What was I before?
What will I be next?
What am I now?
Cruel answer carried in the jesting mind of a careless God.
I will not bend and grovel
When I die. If He says my sins are myriad
I will ask why He made me so imperfect
And he will say "My chisels were blunt."
I will say "Then why did you make so many of me."

—Spike Milligan[21]

Most of us, like the author of this poem, have struggled with the question of the meaning of life. It is a question we are all faced with at some point in our lives—a question we must answer for ourselves.

The meaning of one's life can be elusive and difficult to articulate, and we all find meaning in our lives in many different ways.

What does your life mean? What is the meaning of human life in general?

Do you have a philosophy of life? What is it?

Some people find meaning in their families and their children; others find meaning in their work in the world. People find meaning in religion—in living out their faith. People can find their meaning in service to others, in art, in learning, in creativity—in many different ways. How have you found meaning in your life?

Have you ever found life to be meaningless? Did it fill you with despair? Did you come to some existential understanding? How? What restored the meaning to your life?

What kinds of values were you taught as a child? How have those values changed?

What sorts of religious traditions were there in your home? Have you carried them on? Why or why not?

Have you ever had a religious experience? What were you doing and where did it happen? How did it affect you?

What symbols, either religious or secular, are significant for you? Why?

Do you find meaning in the ideas of social justice, posterity, or the brotherhood of man? How do you act on these ideas?

What kinds of goals do you have in your life—material, social, personal, universal, moral, religious—and how important are they to you? Have your goals always been the same? How have they changed?

Is there one event in your life that is symbolic of your life's meaning? What was it and why is it significant?

How would you characterize your Christian faith? How does it shape your values?

How does your faith give meaning to your life? How does it help you in interpreting life events? Could you give some examples?

Exercise: Night

Elie Wiesel describes his personal crisis of faith, as a young boy facing the horrors of the concentration camp:

> Never shall I forget that night, the first night in camp, which has turned my life into one long night, seven times cursed and seven times sealed. Never shall I forget that smoke. Never shall I forget the little faces of the children, whose bodies I saw turned into wreaths of smoke beneath a silent blue sky. Never shall I forget those flames which consumed my Faith forever. Never shall I forget that nocturnal silence which deprived me, for all eternity, of the desire to live. Never shall I forget those moments which murdered my God and my soul and turned my dreams to dust. Never shall I forget these things even if I am condemned to live as long as God Himself. Never.[22]

While most of us have not experienced the depths of evil of

the concentration camps, we may have faced our own abyss and gone through a crisis of faith.

Have you ever had a crisis of faith? Was it prompted by an event or an experience? What was it like? How did you react? What did you do? What was the outcome?

Exercise: Responsibleness

Viktor Frankl is the originator of "logotherapy," a type of therapy which helps people find meaning in their lives. He writes:

> . . .the meaning of life differs from man to man, from day to day and from hour to hour. What matters, therefore, is not the meaning of life in general but rather the specific meaning of a person's life at a given moment. . . .One should not search for an abstract meaning of life. Everyone has his own specific vocation or mission in life; everyone must carry out a concrete assignment that demands fulfillment. Therein he cannot be replaced, nor can his life be repeated. Thus, everyone's task is as unique as is his specific opportunity to implement it.
>
> As each situation in life represents a challenge to man and presents a problem for him to solve, the question of the meaning of life may actually become reversed. Ultimately, man should not ask what the meaning of his life is, but rather must recognize that it is *he* who is asked. In a word, each man is questioned by life; and he can only answer to life by *answering for* his own life; to life he can only respond by being responsible. Thus, logotherapy sees in responsibleness the very essence of human existence.[23]

How do you react to this idea? Does it make sense to you? Is it helpful to you in exploring the meaning of your own life?

Write a page or two in response to Frankl's ideas about the meaning of life.

15

Your Life Line

Plotting your life line on this chart will help you put *all* the events of your life into perspective. It gives you a visual image of the trends or directions in your life.

It is similar to an electrocardiogram, which shows you your heartbeat on paper, plotted out in graph form. Your life line plots the beat of your life on paper, in graph form.

Start at the dot that is labeled "birth." Each year of your life is numbered (1-100) and there is room to label the significant events in your life.

The chart is designed so that you can put the positive events in your life in the top half (above the center line, which is the neutral point), and you can put the negative events in the lower half of the chart.

For instance, if your father died when you were six years old, you would label that event at year six, and the dot marking that event would probably be close to the bottom of the chart. If you broke your arm at age eight, that would probably also be a negative event, but not as negative as the death, so the dot marking the broken arm would be below the neutral line, but maybe just a little below.

Similarly, the positive events in your life would be marked at different heights on the chart, some being more positive than others.

You can mark all the important events in your life on this graph, label the marks, and then connect your marks with a line, moving up and down according to the events.

Once you have completed the life line from birth to your present age, you can look at your life line and notice the direction it moved.

Does your life line have a lot of ups and downs, or does it move in one general direction?

Does your life seem to be getting better all the time? Or do your life events seem to be all downhill as you age?

What was the highest point in your life? What was the lowest?

Was there a point so low that you thought you fell off the bottom of the chart?

Do you have more positive events than negative events?

Are there any plateaus in your life line? Any smooth periods where life seemed to even out for a long period of time, with no highs and lows?

Are you surprised when you look at your life line, this overall picture of your life?

Can you see God at work in your life line? Describe the points where you see God involved in your life events.

Are any of your significant events religious experiences?

Exercise: *My Future*

You might want to try continuing the plotting of your life line into the future. While your life to date is a solid line, you could continue your life line into the future years with a dotted line, somewhat like an uncompleted road drawn on a map.

If you know of certain events coming up in your future, you can plot them on your graph and label them. How does your future look with these events tentatively penciled in? Do you think your life line will continue in a generally positive direction? Do you foresee a lot of ups and downs? Do you see God at work in your future?

Exercise: *My Tapestry of Life*

To add more detail and perspective to the life line, many life history writers have taken the exercise one step further. Rather than having all their life events plotted on one line, they did different lines for the different themes in their lives. That is, they still use one graph, one sheet of paper, but they use different colored pens or pencils for the different aspects of life.

For instance, maybe your family line (blue) was moving in very positive directions, while life's work (green) was full of negative events. At the same time, health and body image (red) was having both ups and downs, as was sexual development (orange).

You can use the theme writings that you have from the fourteen previous chapters to plot a different colored line for each aspect of your life. This will give you much more detail in your life line, and enable you to see the rich colors in your life.

Conclusion

The Future—Where Do You Go from Here?

You've finished this book and you've finished writing your life story. Now what? Where do you go from here? What are you going to do with the rest of your life?

Many people find that writing their life story is a very cathartic experience. The process enables them to release pent-up feelings and to work through old conflicts and griefs from the past. This unloading of emotional baggage is a tremendous relief. It provides an opportunity for individuals to move into the future with renewed energy and fresh purpose.

In addition, writing your life story from a Christian perspective helps promote spiritual growth and to strengthen faith. Therefore, you can make decisions with the comfort and security of a firm spiritual grounding.

New directions for the future often become apparent during the life history process. Choices for the future evolve naturally, and the way looks very clear. You may decide to change careers, or go back to school, or change lifestyles as a result of the clarifying process of writing your life story. Or, because of what you have discovered in the writing process, you may decide to recommit yourself to your marriage, to your life's work, or to a friendship.

You have probably experienced a new awareness of time, which can be very valuable. We all have the gift of time—maybe ten years, maybe ten months, maybe ten days. Most of us don't know how long our gift of time is, but we do have a sense that we should make the most of it. God has given us the gift of the future, but it is we who must decide what we will do with our gift.

One way to clarify for yourself what you want to do with the future is to construct a "Scale of Desire"[24] for yourself. This Scale of Desire has four levels:

I. *Wishes*—all those things you idly wish for: a million dollars, to be president, to go to the moon, etc.

II. *Wants*—more selective than wishes, these are the things you seriously desire.

III. *Willing and Deciding*—involves your decision and resolve to go after something.

IV. *Action*—actually moving toward the attainment of one of your desires.

There is a selective screening process involved in this scale of desire. You probably have hundreds or thousands of "Wishes," but many of them are simply idle fantasies. Only some of them move up to the next level of "Wants." You don't actually want everything you wish for. You may wish for a million dollars, but you actually want to go back to school. Wants are more concrete and realistic than wishes.

The third level, "Willing and Deciding," involves even fewer items, because you may want something, but never make the decision to go after it. And the last level, "Action," has fewer items still, because taking action on a desire involves commitment of time, energy, and resources.

To help you sort out what you want to do with your life, you can construct your own Scale of Desire for each of the theme areas in your life. For example:

My Scale of Desire for Family

Wishes: _____

_____

_____

_____

_____

Wants: _____

_____

_____

_____

Willing
and
Deciding: _____

_____

Action: _____

My Scale of Desire for Spiritual Life
Wishes: _____
            _____
            _____
            _____
            _____
            _____

Wants: _____
            _____
            _____
            _____

Willing
and
Deciding: _____
            _____
Action: _____

My Scale of Desire for My Life's Work
Wishes: _____
            _____
            _____
            _____
            _____

Wants: _____
            _____
            _____

Willing
and
Deciding: _____
            _____
Action: _____

With different charts for your various desires, you can easily see how much progress you're making at any time. You might be involved with action in your family life, while you haven't gone beyond the wish stage in your life's work, or vice versa.

Writing your Scale of Desire, or several Scales of Desire, can help you to clarify your goals in life and will move you along in a more focused manner.

It is important, of course, to be open to divine guidance in the process. Sometimes our earthly desires interfere with, or sidetrack us from our spiritual desires and growth. We Christians must be especially sensitive to this as we try to keep the various aspects of our lives in harmony. Our Spiritual Scale of Desire should be the most important one, and it should guide and inform our other desires.

Where you go from here is a very personal question that only you can answer. I hope this book and the life history process have helped you to understand and accept your past and to experience the peace of mind that comes with reconciliation. You also have an appreciation of the gift of time, so that you are motivated to make the most of every day, beginning today. Just as you make decisions about how you want to invest your money, you can also decide how you want to invest your time. How you invest yourself (your time and energy and love) can pay off in bountiful terms for yourself and the people you love.

Most importantly, you can decide how you are going to respond to the love that God has shown you in the past. You can use the future to make your faith a living faith, putting into daily practice the joy, peace, and love that are the hallmarks of the Christian faith. You can share your hope with the hopeless. You can bring reconciliation to the estranged. You can make the message of Christ's love real for another person. In short, you can use what you've learned about yourself in the life history process to live a fuller, richer life and to share your blessings with others.

Your future is full of possibilities. You can build on your new self-knowledge and renewed faith to live with peace of mind, in greater harmony with the world and with God.

Appendix A

Suggestions for Use in Groups

Benefits of Doing Life History in Groups

Using the life history technique in group settings has several positive results. Individuals who share their life stories with each other learn to appreciate the uniqueness of each life, while at the same time they see the similarities, the common human bonds that unite us. While no two lives are alike (I like to think of them as "human snowflakes"), they do share certain kinds of experiences and emotions. For instance, the story behind every divorce is different, but the feelings of loss and pain and anger and despair are very much the same. By sharing life stories, people perceive both the uniqueness and the similarities of the human experience.

Individuals can also help each other analyze their lives. When you share your life story with another, often that person will have insights that you may have missed. This helpful sharing of insights contributes further to self-understanding.

Empathy develops when painful experiences are related in a group situation. You feel close to other people when you find out that they have some of the same problems and struggles you do. Hope is instilled when you hear the way someone with a similar problem has solved it or overcome it.

You may gain further insight into yourself by hearing the stories of others. There is the shock of recognition as you see yourself in others.

Sharing life stories is a valuable interpersonal learning experience as you receive feedback on how you are perceived by other people.

Family reenactment often occurs in small groups when the participants are of different ages. This can be a very valuable exercise for those who are struggling to come to terms with old family issues remaining from childhood.

People of different ages who share their life stories are contributing greatly to intergenerational continuity or bridging the generation gap. In one class, I heard a young woman in her early thirties say to a woman in her seventies, "You know, I was so relieved to hear your story, because I always thought it was *my* generation that invented social problems— homosexuality, alcoholism, drugs, etc. It's kind of comforting to know that those things have been going on for a long time, and it's not just us!" Seeing the commonalities between generations can bring parent and child, parent and grandparent, closer together.

The use of life history techniques in church groups can accelerate the process of people getting to know each other, as in new-member classes. In Bible study groups it can demonstrate how biblical principles relate to real-life situations. And in other kinds of small groups, it can provide a whole new perspective for people who thought they already knew each other, thereby renewing, refreshing, and strengthening their friendship. After one particular class conducted in an adult Christian education program, a man came up to me and, pointing to his friend, said, "You know, I have been in the same small group with this guy for the last three years. But I just learned more about him in the last twenty minutes than I have in three years!" His face was aglow with the excitement of *really* getting to know his old friend!

The life history technique can be adapted for use in group counseling situations, especially for people going through life transitions who need a somewhat structured method for sorting out issues and feelings.

In short, the life history process outlined in this book is valuable for individuals to use on their own to gain personal insight and to work toward spiritual growth, and its value is enhanced when used in group settings. The writing process helps integrate one's life and promotes self-acceptance, while the sharing process promotes a feeling of closeness to other people.

Structure, Size, Time, and Logistics

Life history writing can be done with any size group, from four or five people to a hundred or more. This is possible because the sessions are conducted in two parts. The entire group hears a lecture and/or participates in a discussion of the general ideas in the first half of this book; then the group breaks into small discussion groups to talk about each of the theme writing assignments. (The writing, of course, is done outside the group.)

The group can meet on a variety of schedules—anywhere from one to fifteen times, depending on the purpose of the group and the desires of its members. A group that meets only once might want to hear the group leader talk about the writing process and life span development (chapters 2 and 3 of section I) and then break into small groups to work on the life line assignment (chapter 15 in section II).

A group that meets six times could have the leader use each chapter in the first part of the book as a lecture, and have the small groups discuss the theme writings, using whichever six seem most appropriate.

Life history groups can meet daily for two weeks for an intensive experience; or they can meet once a week for ten weeks, which allows more time for writing and reflection.

In a two-day retreat setting, the group leader might select four themes and have participants meet in the mornings for two hours and in the afternoons for two hours, allowing sufficient time between sessions for writing.

Group leaders can also supplement their lectures with additional material (Bible chapters, etc.) to change the emphasis for different purposes.

Time constraints will govern how much time is spent on lecture and how much in the small groups. In a six-week, two-hour class, you can divide each session in half, spending the first half on lecture, the second half in small groups. If each class only meets for an hour, you might want to spend the time half and half, or two-thirds and one-third.

The size of the small discussion groups is important and should be governed by the amount of time available. If the small groups meet for twenty minutes, there should be no more than three people per group. If the groups have an hour for discussion, the optimum size is five or six people. There should never be more than six people per group, since there will not be enough time for all participants to share their stories, and someone will feel slighted when the time runs out.

It is important that all participants agree to share the time equally. Each person should have enough time to read his or her written assignment, with a couple minutes for discussion after each. Sometimes it is helpful to have the group facilitator or a group member act as timekeeper for the group.

When the large group breaks into smaller groups, it is a good idea to separate husbands and wives so they're in different groups, and the same holds true for close friends. They will feel more comfortable in sharing if they do not have to be concerned with what a spouse or a close friend is thinking.

When dealing with a group of people of different ages, the leader should try to distribute the ages between groups as evenly as possible, so all the older people are not in one group and all the younger people in another. Also make sure that men and women are distributed evenly. There will usually be more women than men in a life history class, and one should try to put at least one man in every small group, if possible. This kind of heterogeneous grouping will give more variety to the groups and add richness to the discussion.

Small groups can be conducted with or without group facilitators. If a life history class is offered in a church on a weekly basis with small groups of three, there is no need to have a facilitator for each little group. However, if the life history class is done on an intensive basis, or in an intensive retreat, it is probably good to have a facilitator for each group. The facilitator is not a full participant; rather, he or she is present to keep the discussion flowing smoothly, to provide additional insight, analysis, support, comfort, guidance, and structure, as needed by the group. The facilitator can also take appropriate action if certain issues are too sensitive for someone or if the emotional response to the past is too strong. Sometimes people sign up for life history classes when what they really need is professional therapy. The facilitator can gently counsel such a person to move out of the group and into individual therapy if necessary. (This is actually a rare occurrence but important for group leaders and group facilitators to be aware of.)

Participants should be informed of all the ground rules at the outset of the program, including writing assignments, time, confidentiality, etc. One ground rule is that everyone should *write,* not just tell his or her story. The writing process is a critical aspect of personal integration and insight. Unless one is working with individuals who can't write due to incapacity (blindness, arthritis, etc.) or one is interested in using the themes for reminiscence rather than life history, (which also works very well), all participants should be strongly encouraged to write. Two pages per theme is a good rule of thumb for most groups.

It should also be stated at the outset that life history is not therapy, although it has some therapeutic results. Unless it is used by a professional therapist in a clinical setting, it should not be represented as therapy. An inexperienced or unqualified leader can very quickly encounter more emotional and psychic distress than he or she is equipped to handle.

Professional therapy is problem-centered, designed for individuals with major life problems. Life history provides insight and personal growth to individuals, but it is not problem-centered. It can be very helpful to people in times of transition, and it may be used as an adjunct to therapy, but it should not be used in place of therapy for people who have serious personality problems.

Confidentiality, Trust, and Privacy

Confidentiality and trust are the cornerstones of this life history process conducted in groups. The leader should emphasize this point right from the start. If participants are to share intimate aspects of their lives with other people, they must first feel they can trust those people. They need to know that their stories will not become part of church or neighborhood gossip. This is especially true in church settings and in other groups where people will continue to associate after the life history class or group is finished.

Just as people on airplanes will often share their most intimate secrets with complete strangers, people in life history groups will often share more completely when they are in a group of strangers whom they may never see again. Therefore, it is extremely important that the rule of confidentiality within each small group is stated clearly from the outset.

Participants need to know that their stories will be received in a warm, supportive environment and that they will not be subject to judgmentalism or ridicule when they share their lives. After all, individuals are placing pieces of themselves out on the table for others to see, and this can only be done in an atmosphere of trust. Criticism of another person's story is absolutely forbidden!

Each person should also have the right to privacy, to not share a particular theme with the group if the topic is too sensitive or painful. This only happens occasionally, since most people who sign up for a life history group are more than ready to share. But when people do express a desire to "pass" on a given subject, their wishes should be respected by their small group. No one should feel forced to share everything.

Emotions

While many people become alarmed or concerned at the strong expression of such feelings as anger or grief or pain, especially when these involve tears, in the context of a life history class these emotions are to be expected and accepted as normal human responses to certain life events.

Tears can be cleansing and cathartic, and often a very healthy way for people to release pent-up feelings. The small groups should respond to tears with understanding, patience, and love. As people touch on old wounds, disappointments, and losses, it is natural that some pain might be felt. Each participant should know that it's OK to cry, and the small groups should bear with the person until the crying is under control.

Tears and emotions can be very positive for the group because they help build trust and establish bonds among the members, letting everyone know it's OK to be human, to feel pain, and to share that pain with others.

Only if the crying or emotional outburst is excessive or uncontrollable should the small group facilitator step in and take control of the situation. If there is no facilitator, another group member should assume responsibility.

Possible Problems:

1. *Time.* This is usually the most common problem for small groups. One person will want to talk endlessly (time-hogging), or five out of six of the small group members will talk a little too long, leaving no time for number six. This can be avoided if there is a timekeeper for the group and if everyone knows at the outset that they have X amount of time. Fairness should be stressed, so that everyone has roughly equal time.

The group leader should also make sure, if he or she is giving a lecture before the small groups meet, that the lecture does not run over into small-group time. Participants love their time in small groups and will be upset if they don't have enough time to talk.

2. *Judgmentalism.* This is an absolute no-no! Nothing can make the group fail faster than someone criticizing another person's life. Lives should be treated with respect and understanding. We are all human, and we've all made mistakes and done dumb things or even terrible things. A critical attitude on anyone's part will hurt people's feelings, destroy trust, and inhibit the group process.

3. *"Therapeutic Sophisticates."* Very often, people who have had a lot of therapy will try to act as analyst or therapist for the group. This must be actively discouraged by the large group leader and/or by the small group facilitators. Overanalysis makes others feel self-conscious or defensive. People who are professional counselors, clinicians, and ministers sometimes fall into the trap of trying to act out their professional roles, and may challenge the group leader or facilitator when they should really relax and enjoy themselves as participants. A troublesome individual who is either a therapeutic sophisticate or an actual therapist should be gently but firmly discouraged from overanalyzing other people's lives. (This can be done during the group meeting, or at another time, if necessary.)

4. *Emotions.* One of the most frequent questions I'm asked is about the possibility of a participant being emotionally devastated or unable to handle the flood of memories and feelings that come with an examination of the past. In my experience, this is a very rare occurrence. If the life history group is voluntary, then the people who sign up are ready to share and generally in good mental health. A person who feels the need to deny or repress the past, or someone who is emotionally brittle will not be likely to attend a life history program in the first place. Most people know when they're ready to write and talk about the past, and they know how much they can handle.

In the rare case when someone does become overwhelmed by pain or grief or emotional distress, that person should be assured that it is OK to drop out of the group and he/she may be referred to a professional counselor.

5. *Pathology or Deviance.* Occasionally a group will have a member whose life is so bizarre or traumatic that it seems pathological. Sometimes this is a problem for the group, but it is

surprising how much deviance the groups can handle, especially in a warm, supportive environment. Most groups will be tolerant of the strange person and will exhibit great patience and understanding. This is especially true in a Christian community, where love of neighbor is an important value. The group may exert subtle pressure to rein in the deviant's excessive tales of woe or overwhelming personality. In such situations, group leaders should be watchful and mindful of everyone's rights and needs, but it is not usually cause for alarm or action.

How to End the Groups

Ending the life history groups is always difficult. Participants have come to know each other intimately and the bonding process makes them not want to let go of each other. In fact, sometimes small groups will continue to meet for fellowship long after the life history process is complete.

One good way to ease the sadness of ending is to have a celebration at the last group meeting—with wine or soda, cheese, fruit, and homemade bread or other goodies. The pot-luck feast symbolizes the sharing process that's been going on, and gives everyone the opportunity to contribute his or her specialty.

This breaking of bread is a fitting end to the experience, serving as a celebration of lives as they have been lived. The final theme assignment is on the meaning of life, and it is an appropriate accompaniment to the feast.

The festivities of sharing a meal together help ease the sadness of parting and make closure easier to achieve.

Another exercise to include is to have each person write out a wish for each member of his or her small group and bring these wishes on the last day. The wishes are on separate pieces of paper, folded to ensure privacy, or rolled into little scrolls. Some groups choose to read them aloud to each other, while others read their wishes privately. It is a beautiful, yet simple and inexpensive way for participants to give each other a gift. The gift is a wish—for something that person needs, or wants, or is searching for. You may wish a person success on a specific project, or the discovery of a new love, or the healing of a troubled relationship. By the time a life history group ends (if it has met more than once), each person in the small groups knows the others well enough to make a good wish for each.

It is sometimes appropriate for participants to exchange phone numbers and addresses if they want to keep in touch. It's also fun to schedule a reunion the following year, to see how each other's lives have progressed. Different ideas are appropriate for different groups.

The important thing in ending the life history groups is to reaffirm each individual's life, to celebrate God's love for human beings, and to send participants off into the future with renewed energy and clearer perspective. A pot-luck feast on the last day will help set the right tone and enable everyone to leave with a positive, uplifted feeling.

Appendix B

Telling Your Story

Life History for Personal Insight and Spiritual Growth

The focus of this course is twofold. It promotes (1) self-understanding and an appreciation of the uniqueness and diversity of individual lives, as well as (2) a sense of the common features which characterize all human lives and the relatedness of human beings in their life experiences. As children of God we are all unique, valuable persons with distinctive personalities and styles—no two are alike. At the same time, we are united by the common bonds of humanity—birth and death, love and loss, joy and sorrow. Through our uniqueness come individuality and specialness. Through our common experiences come empathy and closeness.

In order to explore both uniqueness and similarity, the course will be divided into two components. The first segment, in lecture format, will present material from a variety of fields which will serve as tools and guides in the exploration of one's own life, promoting both insight and integration. The second segment will involve small discussion groups where individual lives may be shared and discussed as part of the growth process.

To prepare for these small groups, participants will write two or three pages each week on selected autobiographical themes. Writing is a crucial part of "pulling it all together," and it insures some quiet times for reflection, feeling, and reaction to various life experiences. All participants are strongly urged to spend a little time each week writing. You will get more out of the autobiographical process if you put more in—your life is important!

Week 1

Lecture:

—introductions

—overview of course: goals, purposes, methods, structure, expectations

—Why write? Oral history vs. autobiography

—sensitizing exercises: learning and trying new ways to think about yourself

Assignment for next week: List and briefly describe the major branching points in your life; God's plan for your life; God's interventions in your life. Try doing a life line or life map. (No small group meeting this first day.)

Week 2

Lecture:

—developmental exchange

—relationships

—bonding, attachment

Small Groups: Discuss family history.

Assignment for next week: Write the history or autobiography of your family of childhood and your family of adulthood; God the Father; family celebrations; family conflicts and divisions; family pictures.

Week 3

Lecture:

—history of autobiography

—Christianity and autobiography

—St. Augustine's *Confessions*

—changing concepts of self: objective vs. subjective

Small Groups:Discuss family history.

Assignment for next week: Write the history of your life's work or career. Has it changed? The notion of a calling; God's work; Christianity in the marketplace.

Week 4

Lecture:

—different ways to write about yourself

—styles and techniques

—points of view

—*how* you say things conveys a message, too

—metaphor

Small Groups:Discuss career history.

Assignment for next week: Write about your health history and your body image. Images of beauty, health, strength; the body as temple; the meaning of illness and pain.

Week 5
Lecture:
—identity
—moral development
—images of God
—prayer
Small Groups: Discuss health and body image.

Assignment for next week: Describe the history of your moral development. Who first taught you right from wrong? How have those notions changed?

Week 6
Lecture:
—developmental theories in psychology
—the fabric of life
Small Groups: Discuss history of moral development.

Assignment for next week: Describe the history of your sexual development and your changing sexual roles: what it means to be created male or female.

Week 7
Lecture:
—maturity and mental health
—wisdom
Small Groups: Discuss sex and sex role history.

Assignment for next week: Write about your experiences with death and/or your changing concepts of death. Deaths of others, pets, loved ones, strangers, friends, wartime; confronting your own death; the meaning of death.

Week 8
Lecture:
—prospects for personal change
—free will
—autobiography as insight

Small Groups: Discuss death experiences.
Assignment for next week: Write the history of your heroes. Religious or philosophical heroes; biblical heroes; literary heroes; television or movie heroes; political heroes; personal or family heroes.

Week 9
Lecture:
—life review, reconciliation
—integration, fulfillment
—negatives and positives of life
—owning your life
—knowing yourself
—accepting others
—grace
—forgiveness
Small Groups: Discuss heroes.
Assignment for next week: Write the history of your loves and hates.

Week 10
Lecture:
—meaning of life
—values
—hope
—faith
—important symbols
—contexts of meaning
Small Groups: Discuss loves and hates.
Assignment for next week: Write about your personal philosophy, the meaning of your life. How have your values changes through your life? Has the meaning of your life changed?

Week 11
Lecture:
—the future—now what?
—Where do you go from here?
—goals
—Where do you leave your life?
Small Groups: Discuss values, personal philosophy, meaning of life.
—*Celebration!*

Bibliography

Allport, Gordon W. *The Use of Personal Documents in Psychological Science.* New York:Social Science Research Council, 1942.

Augustine. *Confessions,* tr. by Rex Warner. Mentor Books, 1963.

Baruch, Joel. "Combat Death" in *Death and the College Student,* ed. by Edwin Shneidman. Behavioral Publications, 1972.

Buhler, C. "The Curve of Life as Studied in Biographies," in *Journal of Applied Psychology,* 1935.

Butler, Robert. "The Life Review: An Interpretation of Reminiscence in the Aged," in *Middle Age and Aging,* ed. by Bernice Neugarten. University of Chicago Press, 1968.

Ellis, Albert. *A Guide to Rational Living.* Prentice-Hall, 1961.

Erikson, Erik. *The Life Cycle Completed.* Norton, 1982.

Frankl, Viktor. *Man's Search for Meaning.* Pocket Books, 1963.

Frenkel, E. "Studies in Biographical Psychology," in *Character and Personality,* 1936.

Gould, Roger. *Transformations: Growth and Change in Adult Life.* Simon and Schuster, 1978.

Harding, Goodwin. "Monolithic Daddyism: An Autobiographical Account of Death" in *Death and the College Student.*

Jahoda, M. *Current Concepts of Positive Mental Health.* Basic Books, 1958.

Keen, Sam, and Anne Valley Fox. *Telling Your Story: A Guide to Who You Are and Who You Can Be.* Signet Books, 1973.

Lasch, Christopher. *The Culture of Narcissism.* Norton, 1979.

Levinson, D. J. *et al. The Seasons of a Man's Life.* Knopf, 1978.

Lyons, Robert, *Autobiography: A Reader for Writers.* Oxford University Press, 1977.

Maslow, Abraham. *Motivation and Personality.* Harper & Row, 1954.

Milligan, Spike. *Small Dreams of A Scorpion.* Penguin Books, 1973.

Olney, J. *Metaphors of Self: The Meaning of Autobiography.* Princeton University Press, 1972.

Peck, Robert. "Psychological Developments in the Second Half of Life," in *Middle Age and Aging.*

Piaget, Jean. *The Construction of Reality in the Child.* Basic Books, 1954.

Riegel, Klaus. "Adult Life Crises: Interpretation of Development" in *Life Span Development Psychology: Normative Life Crises.* Academic Press, 1975.

————————— *Foundations of Dialectical Psychology.* Academic Press, 1979.

Sheehy, Gail. *Passages: Predictable Crises of Adult Life.* E. P. Dutton, 1976.

Vaillant, George. *Adaptation to Life.* Little, Brown, 1977.

Whitehead, Evelyn E. and James D. *Christian Life Patterns: The Psychological Challenges and Religious Invitations of Adult Life.* Doubleday Image Books, 1982.

Wiesel, Elie. *Night.* Avon Books, 1969.

Wrightsman, Lawrence. "Personal Documents as Data for Conceptualizing Adult Personality Development." Presidential Address to the Society of Personality and Social Psychology, 1980.

Notes

1. See Gail Sheehy, *Passages: Predictable Crises of Adult Life*. Dutton, 1976.

2. Adapted from Erik Erikson, *The Life Cycle Completed*. Norton, 1982.

3. See Evelyn E. Whitehead and James D. Whitehead, *Christian Life Patterns: The Psychological Challenges and Religious Invitations of Adult Life*. Doubleday, 1982.

4. Adapted from Roger Gould, *Transformations: Growth and Change in Adult Life*. Simon & Schuster, 1978.

5. Adapted from Abraham Maslow, *Motivation and Personality*. Harper & Row, 1954.

6. See Christopher Lasch, *The Culture of Narcissism*. Norton, 1979.

7. Adapted from Lawrence Wrightsman, "Personal Documents as Data in Conceptualizing Adult Personality Development." Presidential Address to the Society of Personality and Social Psychology, September, 1980.

8. Adapted from M. Jahoda, *Current Concepts of Positive Mental Health*. Basic Books, 1958.

9. Adapted from George Vaillant, *Adaptation to Life*. Little, Brown, 1977.

10. Adapted from Robert Butler, "The Life Review: An Interpretation of Reminiscence in the Aged," in Bernice Neugarten, ed., *Middle Age and Aging*. University of Chicago Press, 1968.

11. Viktor Frankl, *Man's Search for Meaning*. Pocket Books, 1963.

12. Klaus Riegel, "Adult Life Crises: A Dialectic Interpretation of Development," in *Life Span Developmental Psychology: Normative Life Crises*. Academic Press, 1975.

13. Adapted from Jean Piaget, *The Construction of Reality in the Child*. Basic Books, 1954.

14. Adapted from Robert Peck, "Psychological Developments in the Second Half of Life," in Neugarten, *Ibid.*

15. See Albert Ellis, *Guide to Rational Living.* Prentice-Hall, 1961.

16. Adapted from Roger Gould, *Ibid.*

17. Sam Keen and Anne Valley Fox, *Telling Your Story: A Guide to Who You Are and Who You Can Be.* Signet, 1973.

18. Adapted from Keen and Fox, *Ibid.*

19. Goodwin Harding, "Monolithic Daddyism: An Autobiographical Account of Death," in Edwin Schneidman, ed., *Death and the College Student.* Behavioral Publications, 1972, p. 91.

20. Joel Baruch, "Combat Death," in *Ibid.,* p. 37.

21. Spike Milligan, "Me," in *Small Dreams of a Scorpion.* Penguin Books, 1973, p. 28.

22. Elie Wiesel, *Night.* Avon Books, 1969.

23. Viktor Frankl, *Ibid.,* pp. 171-173.

24. Adapted from Keen and Fox, *Ibid.,* p. 104.